THE CRUCIAL 12

Powerful Insights for Marketing Leadership

THE CRUCIAL 12

Powerful Insights for
Marketing Leadership

STEVE WOLGEMUTH

www.BookpressPublishing.com

Published in Des Moines, Iowa, by:

Bookpress Publishing
P.O. Box 71532
Des Moines, IA 50325
www.BookpressPublishing.com

Publisher's Cataloging-in-Publication Data

Names: Wolgemuth, Steven R., author.
Title: The Crucial 12 : powerful insights for marketing leadership / Steve Wolgemuth.
Description: Des Moines, IA: Bookpress Publishing, 2019.
Identifiers: LCCN 2019941510 | ISBN 978-1-947305-03-8
Subjects: LCSH Marketing--Management. | Success in business. | Leadership. | Selling. | Branding (Marketing) | BISAC BUSINESS & ECONOMICS / Marketing / General
Classification: LCC HF5415 .W658 2019 | DDC 658.8--dc23

First Edition
Printed in the United States of America
10 9 8 7 6 5 4 3 2 1

Before this dedication is dismissed by the reader as just another sappy tribute, I'd like to point out the hundreds of days my team has covered for me at work while I was out of the office, writing this book. I'd like to mention the countless days, over this two-year journey, my beautiful wife patiently entertained herself for days at a time, as I sat alone and wrote this during what normal couples would have called, "vacations." There's also that extra help I required of my incredibly helpful writing coach, Anthony Paustian, who had no idea what he was taking on when he offered to work with me. These selfless supporting acts flowed naturally from the admirable characters of these people, and I'm blessed beyond measure to have them in my life.

CONTENTS

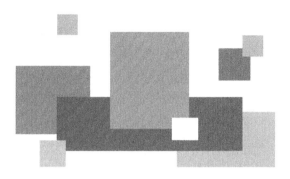

Why?

Why does marketing succeed under some leaders but not others? Most would assume it has to do with how much money is spent or the talent level of the marketing professionals involved. Certainly, these may be factors, but after running an agency for more than a decade and consulting with hundreds of leaders, I came to another conclusion. *A leader's behavior affects marketing outcomes.* This nugget of insight is part of what compelled me to write this book.

There is no shortage of books on leadership, but if I search for books specifically about how to *lead* marketing, the results are disappointing. Instead, I find books that attempt to teach leaders to be marketing experts. I've read many of these books, and while most are brilliant, they're written for scrappy entrepreneur types, marketers, and leaders who are keenly interested in marketing.

The problem is most business leaders don't share that interest, and they don't have the time, education, or core competency to become marketing experts. To make matters worse, marketing has never been more complicated. Competitive forces and fast-changing technology platforms have made marketing success a daunting responsibility. It's no wonder business leaders, especially small business leaders managing many different concerns, don't have the needed clarity about how to invest their marketing resources effectively. Frankly, most would prefer not to have the responsibility because it's simply not their thing. Expecting them to become marketing experts is not the solution.

Most leaders don't want to become marketers. And they shouldn't. Nor should they feel guilty about their lack of passion in this crucial aspect of business management. But in the end, they may have to live with the outcomes of poor marketing: lost opportunities, competitors moving ahead, and wasted marketing dollars. Ignoring marketing isn't the answer.

Then what is the solution for leaders today? I'm convinced they must learn to *lead* marketing efforts from a high level. *Marketing leadership is the art and science of directing, managing, and even inspiring great work from marketing employees, subcontractors, and agencies.* Leaders must learn how to play that role.

I wrote *The Crucial 12* as a guide for business leaders who want to develop their marketing leadership skills. In it, readers will discover and unpack the essential questions they must ask, questions that will create focus around key areas, inform decisions, and direct marketing strategies.

I make no apologies in saying *The Crucial 12* is not a marketing book, and marketing experts who read it might be disappointed. It is a leadership book that outlines a vital thought paradigm that even non-marketers can use to direct their marketing stakeholders and inspire them to do their best work.

Years ago, I was asked to serve on the board of directors for a private college. I felt the other members were of higher social or financial standing than I was, so I felt humbled by this appointment and somewhat inadequate. When I asked the college president how I could bring the most value to the school, his answer was immediate and brilliant. "Ask good questions," he advised. He knew I had that capability, and that would make me the most valuable to his leadership team.

You will bring more value to your team of marketers as you improve your ability to ask good questions. If you ask the right questions, you'll draw focus to the right issues. This book is organized to help you do just that.

By the time you finish this book, you will have a framework for how to think about marketing at a higher strategic level and tools for identifying priorities, holding everyone accountable, and developing a culture rooted in marketing improvement. Armed with these questions, you will recognize the significant role you must play to facilitate positive marketing outcomes and how to draw out the best from the talented marketers on your team.

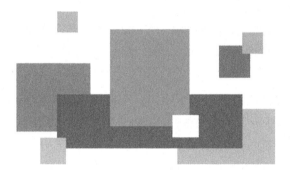

The Epidemic of Bad Leadership

Peter's Story

Peter was the CEO of a pool and spa company with five locations and 45 full-time employees. He was naturally energetic, a competent leader, and loved coming to work every day, until recently.

Sales were down. They had been on a downward trend for the last two years. Up to this point, he could ignore the sales slump, dismissing it as "a slow season that will rebound." But lately, his inner voice was telling him, "This isn't going to turn around on its own." Peter's company was losing market share to competitors, and he knew he could no longer ignore it.

Frankly, Peter didn't know what to do. Nothing he had tried had worked. He had done an exemplary job at identifying all the outside factors that had led to this: more competitors offering cheaper products, and the economic downturn he believed might have been hurting pool sales in general. But he felt powerless to fix it.

Peter was waking up at night, thinking about how he might

have to lay off some employees in the coming months. How would he be able to face their families? If he didn't turn this around, it could have unthinkable long-term effects for the employees who had worked for the company their entire lives. The stakes were high. Peter needed to get to the bottom of why his marketing wasn't working.

He had hired, and subsequently fired, three marketing companies in three years. Each of them had used up significant marketing budgets, but none of them had helped increase sales. Over that same time period, Peter had gone through two different marketing directors internally. Even after 18 months, neither one of them had been able to increase sales numbers or even keep pace with the growth of their competition. To this point, Peter had done a good enough job comforting his employees, family, and colleagues as to why sales were down. He had convinced everyone but himself that this was a normal and temporary decline in sales. But Peter knew his competitors were gaining market share, and he couldn't figure out why. It was wearing on him.

Peter was finding it increasingly difficult to be excited about going to work, a new emotion to him. It was disorienting, and it was starting to affect his confidence and his ability to concentrate.

Why was this happening? Peter ran a tight ship. Their financials were in order, and he knew how every dollar moved through his organization. Operations were stellar. Peter loved the pool and spa business and knew it better than anyone.

And Peter loved challenges—a difficult customer, a negotiation with a manufacturer, deciding which hot tubs to stock the coming year, hiring and firing—he was a master with those issues. It gave him the energy to tackle challenges that would cripple most leaders.

The fact was, he felt much more comfortable solving more exacting issues, like cash and inventory management, than tackling the complicated issues of marketing and business development. Like many leaders today, Peter felt insecure when working on marketing-related tasks for his businesses, and the internet made his insecurity even worse. He wasn't as tech-savvy as he wanted to be. Peter blamed the business down-turn on his "bad hiring decisions," but inside, Peter felt responsible. When it came to marketing in today's world, Peter felt inadequate.

Adding to the stress, he knew the success or failure of his business's marketing would have a huge impact on his family, not to mention the families of his 45 team members. If he didn't get this business going again, how could he ever look at himself in the mirror?

Most Leaders Prefer Operations Over Marketing

Like Peter, many business leaders sometimes feel they have the weight of the world on their shoulders. That's especially true when things aren't going well. And since marketing is not an exact science, many operations-minded leaders find it frustrating. Like Peter, they believe one simple hire of a marketing firm or an internal marketing director will solve their business marketing problems. Most of the time, it doesn't work that way.

Naive leaders believe marketing is easy and any hired agency or employee can do it. They think marketing is mostly about organizing advertising campaigns. But successful, business-growing marketing is not easy. It requires careful attention to strategy and execution. And business leaders have an ongoing role to play in their company's marketing, one that few leaders are prepared to do well.

Through my role as CEO of the digital marketing company YDOP (which, by the way, stands for "Your Dream, Our Project"), years of speaking engagements in front of business leaders, and sitting across the table from entrepreneurs, business founders, and people in charge of running companies, colleges, and nonprofits, I've had a front-row seat to how leaders approach marketing, and I've observed a clear pattern. Most leaders lack confidence in directing the marketing efforts in their organizations. Worse, they might be blind to their own incompetence, creating chaos, and negatively affecting financial outcomes.

To test my hypothesis, I began asking audiences at my speaking engagements about this topic. At the beginning of my speech, I would say:

> *"I once heard that leading a company involves three categories of activities: Operations, Financial Management, and Marketing/Business Development. I've also heard that few leaders are naturally drawn to all three. Which one or two of these three areas do you feel most confident to lead? In other words, when you come into the office, would you feel most ready to solve a problem related to operations, financial management, or marketing?"*

When I asked for a show of hands, I saw consistent results audience after audience. Most leaders are like Peter. In fact, 85 percent of the leaders I survey prefer to focus on operational or financial management issues over marketing.

I can relate to being strong in some areas and less confident in others. For many years, I was far less confident in managing the financial aspects of my company. When my company was young, I relied on several people to help me: a part-time bookkeeper, a part-time CPA, my business accountant, an employee, and my wife. I was getting nowhere. I left it up to them to figure out how my finances should be put in order. It was a mess. I wanted to implement a profit-sharing program but couldn't because I didn't have an efficient way of determining my monthly profit. I wanted to know the ratio between my payroll and my adjusted gross income but I wasn't able to organize reliable data around that important metric. Out of frustration, I tried to tell them how to do their jobs. But that didn't help at all.

I remember the day when my wife approached me in frustration. "I quit," she said. "I'm not doing this anymore. I'm not qualified to manage our finances the way you want me to."

"You can't quit," I protested. "This is our business!" We found humor in the moment, but we were both at our wits' end. I knew the future of my business would require better financial management and reports each month.

I sought education in this area. Fortunately, I was part of a business network that provided training for leaders. I attended a multiday workshop and came home a changed man. I didn't learn how to do my company's books at that conference; I learned what good management looks like, what good leaders expect, the reports they ask for, and how they put safety checks in place.

I never became a good financial manager, and I didn't learn how to create a balance sheet or set up an accrual system for my company's finances. Leading isn't doing. Instead, I learned which questions good leaders ask their teams. I got greater clarity on what type of team I needed. That education positioned me to make some game-changing leadership decisions. Leaders need vision of what success looks like. Until they have that vision, they will, like me, get nowhere. One cannot lead without vision. Through intentional personal development, I found that needed clarity. Only then could I do what every leader must do well: *articulate a vision and get the right people on board.*

Just as I struggled with financial management, I'm convinced many leaders struggle with marketing and business development. In the midst of that struggle, many leaders succumb to bad leadership practices like impulsive hiring, abdication, or micromanagement. When leaders recklessly hire others to fill in the gap for their lack of vision and high-level oversight, that's not delegation. It's abdication. Successful leaders understand the important role they have in leading marketing success from a higher level, providing clarity, vision, and support. They also understand their own weaknesses and recognize the need to surround themselves with talented people who make up for those weaknesses. That's Leadership 101.

What Bad Delegation Looks Like

Joan, the president of a local private school, and her team recognized they needed a knowledgeable marketing director to help beef up their lead generation. For far too long, their organization didn't have the leadership or a guiding vision for marketing or growing the institution. In fact, all four departments were building their own websites on different platforms with different subcontractors from their own department budgets.

As a vendor for this organization, I had an inside view of the chaos that was created when the leaders made their next move. They hired a talented graphic designer with an impressive resume who could create beautiful brochures, advertisements, and publications. They put him in charge of marketing.

Over the next year, it became apparent that the organization had made a big mistake by impulsively hiring "a marketing person." What they needed was twofold: a unified marketing effort to support one cohesive plan for each of the four departments and an effective presence online so potential customers could find them easily. They'd gotten neither.

This employee didn't have expertise in bringing teams together, working with a digital agency, or writing a comprehensive plan. He was a talented artist, not the marketing coordinator the organization needed. That significant detail was overlooked in the leadership's eagerness to wash their hands of marketing responsibilities. They hired the first person who was "a talented marketer" and a good cultural fit.

Fast-forward two years, and that same organization was again interviewing for the marketing director's now-vacated position. But this time, things were different, as a talented COO had meanwhile filled in as the interim marketing director.

I worked personally with that COO. We first built a vision for the direction of the organization, which was extremely clarifying as we considered the job description. Not surprisingly, the next hire for that position turned out to be a home-run for the organization.

Full of desire to have help with marketing, and lacking vision for that area of their businesses, leaders often make poor hiring decisions. This impulsive, overly-eager hiring is the worst type of abdication. Unfortunately, this happens more often than not.

Bad leaders abdicate. Good leaders delegate. On the surface, the two look similar, because the leader has found *someone* to cover an area of responsibility. The difference lies in the preparation *before* hiring. While it might seem intimidating, a leader must grasp some basic concepts about how to lead their marketing. In the chapters ahead, this book will discuss the perspectives successful marketing leaders have, so readers can gain the confidence and empowerment needed to be brilliant directors of their company's marketing concerns.

Get Out of My Kitchen!

Growing up, I can still hear my mother yelling, "Get out of my kitchen!" We knew exactly what that meant. She had a job to do, and we were getting in her way with our board games and the family dog on the floor under her feet. If we wanted dinner, we needed to give her space and stop frustrating her. That sentiment summarizes otherwise good marketing agencies which end up feeling micromanaged. Like abdication, micromanagement is not good leadership. It's what insecure leaders do to exert power. Micromanagers get in the way. While they may feel as though they are fighting for their company by auditing every penny and every activity they pay vendors to do, the opposite is true.

As I was writing this book, I had to fire a client who came into my office and asked my staff to outline exactly what they had been doing when they were working on his account. He wanted to assess whether or not my team's pace of work was satisfactory. What's sad is he had enjoyed several years of great marketing results from my team. As time went on, his competitors began investing more effort in their online presence while he insisted on scaling back. No matter how hard our team tried to convince him he needed to rebuild his website and engage in some other marketing activities, he pushed back, suspecting we were just trying to get him to spend more.

The fact is, we were. He needed to. His competitive environment had changed. But when traffic to his website started to trend downward (as we predicted), he became a micromanager, thinking the problem might be our productivity, that we didn't work hard enough during the very little time he paid us to engage with his campaign each month. At the end of the day, I wrote his team a farewell message thanking them for their past patronage. We had no choice but to fire the client. His micromanagement style will continue to hurt his business success.

Talented marketers are in demand. They won't continue to work for bad leaders, not as employees or in agencies. But good leaders learn how to bring out the best in a talented employee or agency.

Micromanagement is a terrible approach that never leads to brilliant marketing results—it only gets in the way.

The Epidemic of Bad Marketing Leadership

In preparation for writing this book, I surveyed 40 marketers from 22 agencies across the United States, asking them to share conversations they had with business leaders, specifically about the questions they were asked. The survey results astounded me. Marketing professionals from all across the country expressed the same frustrations about business leaders who interfere with marketing outcomes. Stories included leaders being clueless about marketing strategy, micro-managing budgets, and treating talented and seasoned marketers like temp workers. When it comes to working with an agency or overseeing in-house teams, bad marketing leadership seems both commonplace and predictable.

The Small Business Association reports that about half of new businesses are unable to survive for more than five years. Of those that survive, many more fail before their 10th anniversary. I've often heard this failure rate attributed to a common issue: "running out of cash" before the business becomes profitable. Regardless of how we describe the plight of the small business, one thing is universal. Businesses need a plan to take a product or service to market. Growth depends on successful marketing leadership, a talent I'm convinced is often lacking in business leaders.

Meanwhile, the average annual client turnover rate for agencies in the United States can be 20 percent or higher. That's outrageous and an indication that either leaders are making bad hiring decisions when they choose agencies, or that expectations are not being met. Are so many agencies *that* bad? In my experience, the answer is no, but many agency relationships do go bad.

So what did I learn through my surveys? The survey results echoed my own experiences. I could only conclude that certain bad leadership behaviors were common across the country. The same comments kept coming up when I asked agencies to describe bad clients. "They micromanage," "They don't respond," and "They just don't get it," categorically represented the long list of agency comments about business leaders.

Bad marketing leadership is lethal to a business

Bad leaders are more lethal to their businesses than they realize. Even an established business can fall behind after a short period of bad marketing leadership, missing opportunities for exponential growth, allowing the competition to get ahead.

For a business such as Peter's (the pool and spa company), good reputation and referrals will likely keep it alive through many seasons of marketing negligence. But eventually, those shortcomings will allow competitors to take market share from him. Competitors who gain traction on search engines, build connections, and communicate with their target audiences are better able to execute effective strategies and grow their brand's reputation slowly compared to poorly managed businesses.

New Questions

I've had the privilege of meeting with many interesting leaders over many years to talk about marketing. Most of those meetings came about because of their interest in hiring my team to help them grow their businesses. What's shocking is their lack of skill for having that conversation. I often get the feeling that many leaders are expecting me to provide a "sales spectacle" that will blow them away. I'm convinced many, from their lack of confidence, are meeting with me and my team in hopes of getting talked into something.

Still others come with a history of bad agency relationships. They are jaded and concerned they'll make a wrong agency choice again, so they ask questions like, "What exactly are you going to do?" "How much do you charge?" "Do you work for any of my competitors?" And they make comments to put themselves in a position of power like, "We're talking to several other agencies," and "Put together a marketing plan for us, and we'll see what we think of it."

In my experience, effective leaders engage in a different conversation, and you can judge the sophistication of an effective leader by the questions they ask. They know what to focus on. It follows, then, that a less-experienced and less-effective leader can greatly improve their ability to direct their marketing teams by learning to ask better questions.

This book will cover 12 questions I believe will be transformative for you. Armed with these questions, you'll discover key issues, incorporate the right stakeholders, engage in the best strategies, and pay attention to the metrics that matter most. As a leader, when you ask good questions, you will keep your marketing stakeholders focused on the right things and bring accountability to areas that are truly critical. Your involvement will be transformative to your organization.

CHAPTER SUMMARY

- Most leaders prefer other aspects of business leadership, like operations and financial management, more than marketing, and they aren't prepared to lead their teams effectively.

- Many leaders micromanage their marketing stakeholders or put others in charge and ignore marketing concerns.

- Marketing leadership is crucial to the success of most businesses.

- Leaders can become effective leaders of their business's marketing without becoming marketing experts.

What's Our High-Level Strategy?

Karl was hired three years ago to be the marketing director for a prominent HVAC company. The business served a local market within a 30-mile radius, and they were one of the three largest providers in their territory, specializing mostly in residential heating and air conditioning services.

Lately, Karl was feeling pressure from the company's owners. The competition seemed to be growing faster than they were.

Karl was smart and an excellent communicator. He understood technology, too, and diligently kept their website up-to-date with new and interesting content. In fact, when he first started, Karl had led the implementation of a comprehensive lead-generation system that used written content to attract new customers. Each week, Karl would write helpful articles related to the industry, answering questions customers would commonly ask as they explored HVAC options.

From all of the key performance indicators, it was a success. Tens of thousands of visitors from across the United States were reading Karl's blog posts and articles each month. Some of his articles were re-posted in national publications online. Traffic to their website was off-the-charts compared to their local competitors.

But as they reviewed the number of new leads generated each month, they weren't seeing the business growth they had hoped for. Readers were learning from Karl's articles and, ironically, Karl had even become known as the expert in HVAC marketing. However, Karl's company was simply not doing that well at getting new customers.

One of Karl's competitors was Bonnie, a 30-year-old entrepreneur who started a competing HVAC business just five miles away from Karl's employer. Her company was growing incredibly fast because of some good marketing decisions she was making. In fact, she was taking on new customers at such a rapid pace, she could hardly keep up.

Bonnie spent one-tenth the time and money on her marketing as Karl did, and she had no in-house marketing employees helping her. She had decided early on to outsource that part of her business, but she didn't do it haphazardly. She knew that her business was serving a local audience, and she needed a strategy that leveraged the proximity she had to her audience. With this basic mindset, Bonnie hired a firm that specialized in local business marketing, local SEO, and local websites.

Bonnie had them build a website that would appeal to her local audience. It had pictures that would feel familiar to her clients—her location, her trucks, and her team. She closely monitored how people were navigating the website, which pages they visited, and what actions they took before leaving. From those observations, the marketing company was able to make ongoing adjustments. Within two years, Bonnie began referring to her website as "the conversion machine."

Early on, Bonnie's marketing agency was able to help her dominate local search results. In fact, within a year, Bonnie's company had a great presence on search engine results pages for anyone nearby making HVAC-related searches. She had also outpaced Karl's company in garnering local reviews online. Bonnie's business had a professional presence on every local directory for HVAC companies. Her company had joined local organizations and had their logos on her website as trust symbols. She also had a regular stream of testimonials, both written and video, from local residents who consistently mentioned great customer experiences.

Bonnie implemented a local marketing strategy. Her approach was to create awareness of her company only when and where people were searching for it. She leveraged that awareness with her ubiquitous web presence, designed to get visitors to take action.

In short, her strategy was to capture relevant search traffic and direct those users to her website where they could easily learn about and contact her business. The strategy paid off. Leads were pouring in. Why had Bonnie outpaced Karl's business development? It's simple. Karl chose a valid strategy, using content to position his brand as authoritative. But it wasn't the best one for reaching his local audience. It was a valid strategy, just not the right one. Bonnie chose a strategy that was most effective for her business type.

Most business leaders I encounter are not intentional about strategy. While many leaders insist their companies have written mission statements, few leaders today demand written marketing strategies. In fact, most companies end up unintentionally using a strategy that happens to come along with the marketing company they retain or the marketing director they hire. If a branding agency is hired, a branding strategy is used. If a content marketing company is engaged, a content marketing strategy is deployed. If a social media company is hired, a social media strategy becomes the approach. Most leaders back into strategy.

To be truly effective in leading their organization's business growth, a leader must be intentional about strategy. Backing into a strategy, as Karl's company did, is a formula for spending too much money on long-term disappointment.

What's a Good Strategy?

After more than a decade of marketing consultation with hundreds of leaders, my single most significant and consistent disappointment is that I'm never asked, "What strategy will we use?" I find it disappointing because this, in effect, is an important responsibility a leader has when they consider hiring an agency or when they meet with their in-house marketing staff.

I'm convinced leaders truly believe they are being served with strategy when they aren't. It's understandable because "strategy" is nearly always used in conversations with marketers. They say things like, "We're going to use an email strategy." But email is not a strategy; email is a thing you send to people. I'm sure what they mean is they're going to put careful thought into writing interesting content and sending it to a targeted audience, but that's tactical, not necessarily strategic.

A brilliant marketing strategy is always built on a core insight or insights about the marketing challenges any business or organization is facing. This is why leaders must be involved in high-level marketing conversations; the leader typically ends up discovering key insights that revolutionize their organizations. In Richard Rumelt's excellent book, *Good Strategy/Bad Strategy: The Difference and Why it Matters*, he says a strategy needs to be simple and obvious and able to be described coherently. He advises that, "A leader's most important responsibility is identifying the biggest challenges to forward progress and devising a coherent approach to overcoming them."

Unless your tactics are designed around an organizing strategy, you may not have a great approach. In a competitive world where marketing money and time need to be used as effectively as possible, leaders need to find leverage, and that comes from the hard work of strategy development. A committed leader can learn to discern between a winning strategy and a bad one (or worse, a random execution of tactics) if they start by asking their team to explain it to them in simple terms. If their team can't do that, or if the strategy doesn't align with the business case, the needed timeline, or the intended audience, it isn't the right plan. If it sounds exactly like what everyone else is doing, it's probably not a strategy, and certainly not a great one.

Leaders who abdicate their involvement at a high level often hire "marketing people" to do this part. More often than not, those delegates simply dive into tactical marketing execution. They build a website, they post on Facebook, or they put up a billboard. In the end, the results are mediocre and leaders are justifiably reluctant to increase their marketing budgets.

Rushing into tactical execution, in my experience, is a very common mistake made today, especially in small- and medium-sized business marketing. Experienced marketers and agencies have pet approaches they're accustomed to executing, and they tend to dive right in. Tactical trial and error is not a valid strategy, but in my experience, it's the most-used approach.

Rumelt says, "The core of strategy work is always the same; discovering the critical factors in a situation and designing a way of coordinating and focusing actions to deal with those factors."

Strategies are simple. If they can't be stated in simple terms, they need more thought, or they need to be scaled back to a few core insights. I recommend leaders insist on keeping written strategies in front of all marketing stakeholders as each blog post is written, with each iteration of a website's development, and during each monthly review of metrics. Leaders must demand clarity around strategy.

Three Problems

You might think marketing strategies are complex or difficult to create. They're not. Good strategy always addresses common marketing problems and creates solutions for the three key areas of marketing: *Awareness, Consideration,* and *Decision*. To devise a good marketing strategy, a leader must first reflect on the overarching challenges facing their company in these areas of marketing:

1. *Awareness.* How will strangers discover the brand's product(s) or service(s)?

2. *Consideration.* What do people need to know, feel, and believe in order to move forward?

3. *Decision.* What does the conversion step look like?

Understanding the challenges of these three parts of the marketing funnel is the key to developing and evaluating a successful marketing strategy. *A good plan will have a solution for each of these problems.* It might even involve three separate strategies, one for each part, or it may implement one overarching strategy that solves all three marketing problems.

Solving Our Problem

My digital marketing agency is in a competitive industry. We coexist with a lot of smart-sounding, aggressive competitors who are constantly reaching out to the same businesses that are also our potential customers. These businesses don't trust most of what they hear from agencies which, to them, look and sound very similar. In our industry, creating awareness with these companies in a way that leads to "consideration" is extremely difficult using traditional advertising and direct outreach.

Articulating our problem as such was the key to developing our marketing plan. We clarified our guiding insight—*trust* was the main issue from which to create a strategy. If a lead comes to us with a momentum of trust, they are far more likely to become a client. Rather than using direct marketing or responding to RFPs (Requests for Proposals) as many agencies do, we used other tactics. Our two-fold plan for creating awareness was hosting educational events and building referring partnerships. Both of these approaches not only generated leads, they built trust in our capabilities.

We arranged speaking engagements, lunches, and marketing lectures to our local business community. We also published blog posts and videos to support this educational outreach. Beginning a relationship through education to a targeted audience of potential clients is a great way to establish a level of trust that may lead to a business relationship.

We developed referral programs to be more intentional about meeting potential clients. Clients who already used us were encouraged to make introductions to other potential clients. We forged deeper relationships with other professionals who were able and willing to introduce and recommend us to company-owners and decision-makers when they were looking for digital marketing services.

Getting Started

It's okay if you feel like a deer in the headlights. If you don't spend time in this space, it isn't easy to come up with the best ideas. It's even more difficult to imagine possible scenarios for those less familiar with the internet and the marketing landscape.

The good news is a leader doesn't have to become a marketer to be involved in strategy development. They simply need to make sure the right team is around the table and the hard work of good strategy development is done before tactical discussions get started. Leaders who aren't accustomed to having these conversations might benefit from asking the five questions I've outlined below. I've often used these to reveal pivotal insights, especially when sitting down with leaders, their marketing teams, salespeople, and other stakeholders familiar with business development and marketing.

Assuming you have narrowed down a specific business problem or opportunity you'd like to focus on, and you have clarity around the marketing problem or problems, these questions will help guide a productive conversation.

1. What have we learned so far? What's working?

By default, marketing discussions typically aim to explore new, untried opportunities for business development. Teams want to ask, "What new and unknown thing can we try?" But a smart leader may choose to divert that line of discussion by asking "What is working so far?"

Encouraging businesses to spend time studying their own success may be the single most effective coaching approach I've discovered in marketing consultation. I simply ask, "What's working?" and then, "How can we do more of it?" or "How can we do it *better*?" This approach comes from my underlying admiration and respect for successful business leaders, especially founders and entrepreneurs. The fact is, they've beaten all odds and stayed in business when others haven't. They wouldn't have grown or sustained their companies unless they had some way to attract new clients.

What's most interesting to me about these same leaders is they are typically unaware of how they've become successful. They really have to think about it. But once they do, they find some profound insights. Often core ideas that companies are built on seem like basic common sense to founders. I've found them to be incredibly valuable for developing marketing strategies that are a natural fit for the company and destined to succeed.

For example, when my company realized referrals from trusted sources were our key driver of new business, we leaned into the idea of getting leads from them. From there, we became much more intentional about growing through providing education and building a referral network. The blog writing and social media work were in service to this overarching strategy.

2. What pathway did our customers take?

I sometimes ask clients to envision an ideal customer or a few ideal customers. Then I encourage them to tell a story about how they became customers. How did they first hear about the company? Did they know any other customers? What did they need to know? What did they experience online? What circumstances were driving their decision? Who influenced their decision?

The answer is never just one thing. For example, if they saw an ad in the newspaper and called, that's not the only answer. They probably looked at the website, heard of the business from an existing customer, drove by some business signage, went to an event the business sponsored, and investigated the business last year after finding it on Google. Companies are well-served by doing research and looking for patterns. What seems to work over time? Do you notice any recurring themes? What can you learn about how, when, and why customers choose you, and what experiences do you need to provide for them?

While this line of questioning is similar to the first question—What is working?—it will tend to uncover more tactical successes. It should focus more on users' behaviors and the layers of experiences they had before becoming a customer. We'll discuss this more deeply later in the chapter, "What's the Thing That Sells the Thing?"

3. What drove them to make a decision?

In this part of the discussion, stakeholders are asked to list life circumstances, frustrations, fears, aspirations, and every emotion associated with customer decisions. The insights uncovered in this exercise are often quite informative for teams as they construct and plan the "consideration" and "decision" pieces of the marketing plan. Emotions drive decisions. Clearly understanding what a customer's needs are along the purchase pathway may provide a game-changing insight into how a business constructs the consideration and the decision parts of the strategy.

4. Why didn't the customer follow through?

If the potential customer became aware of a product or service but didn't follow through, what happened? This question will be answered with a mix of research and informed imagination. Both will be helpful.

While this discussion might get tactical and into the weeds of user-experience design, it can also inform a team about a potential overarching strategy. It may uncover an underlying problem that, when solved, will bring great marketing results.

For example, an online shoe retailer was having trouble growing his online sales, even after running many successful awareness campaigns. Web traffic was higher than ever. Through this exercise, he came to realize other online shoe retailers have traditionally made returns complicated and expensive. His buyers were dropping out of their purchase pathway as they remembered those experiences.

With that informed assumption, the online shoe retailer added language on the website that made his no-hassle, free shipping return policy clear to customers. This was again reinforced throughout the checkout process. This change increased sales by 23 percent overnight.

This "pre-mortem" line of questioning may also ask, "If they don't follow through and become our customer, what do they do instead?" Asking the question this way often reveals the real problem the marketing strategy needs to address.

As an example, there was a time in my company's history when we realized our biggest competitor was not another company. It was the customer. Some people we pitched services to didn't hire us because they believed they could do their own internet marketing using their own staff. With that guiding insight, we began making sure potential clients understood more clearly the breadth and complexity of the talent needed to execute successful strategies. We also reminded them how expensive talented marketers are and the cost/benefit analysis of outsourcing this important responsibility to an agency.

5. What questions are people asking?

I'm often surprised how many business leaders and marketers do all their planning without gathering insights from the people who take sales calls. There is no greater resource for gaining key insights about customer mindsets than people who regularly talk to them. This is especially true for developing a strategy around the consideration phase of the marketing strategy.

Years back, I ran an importing agency as a service to dressage horse buyers. After a year of countless hours on the phone with clients, I could predict with great accuracy their questions before they would even ask. "How many days will we be shopping, will we use a European veterinarian to inspect the horse, and how much does it cost to fly the horse back to the US?" I could even predict the order in which they would ask them!

Using that knowledge, I created a private section on my website that was password protected. On that portion of the site, I answered these questions one at a time in the order I knew was typical, each page devoted to answering one question. I not only answered their questions, I also attempted to address their emotional concerns using customer video testimonials on each page. At the bottom of each page, after questions were answered with pictures, links, and testimonials, I'd post the next question with a link to the page that answered the question. Customers told me it was as if I was reading their minds.

Knowing what customers are asking when they call may provide essential insights that a business can use to design a marketing strategy that moves customers from the "awareness" stage through the "consideration" stage and on to a decision.

Is this a Good Strategy?

There's a fair chance any leader following this book's advice will ask their teams, "What's our strategy?" But when they're given an answer, how can they know if it's a good one? What should guide their gut feeling about it? Good strategies have some key elements that set them apart from mediocre approaches. Here are some suggestions for evaluating a strategy.

Look for unique, core insights.

If the strategy is nothing more than an approach just as easily used by another similar company, there's an opportunity to step up the game a bit. It may be the right approach, but it may need to be enhanced. If that's the case, try asking a question like, "How could we execute this strategy in a way our competition couldn't?"

I might also ask, "What do we know about our marketing problem that our competition doesn't understand (as clearly as we do)?" Understanding the true problem to solve is often the most difficult, yet most fundamental part of developing a marketing strategy.

Other helpful questions to help improve or enhance a strategy are, "What information and insights about our specific audience can we use?" and "What have we learned about our customers' buying behaviors?"

Address the three marketing problems.

Just like a chain is only as strong as its weakest link, a marketing strategy is only as effective as its ability to solve all three marketing problems—awareness, consideration, and decision. Sometimes multiple strategies need to work in tandem to create a lead-generation system.

Failing to address all three aspects of marketing is a common blind spot for leaders. This has been made obvious to me time and time again by clients in the last decade. For example, a client might hire our company to do SEO for them. A year later, we've added a significant year-over-year improvement of traffic numbers to their website from quality sources, like people searching for their products or services online. Then they call us in for a meeting and say, "What you're doing isn't working because we're not getting any business from it!"

This is maddening. We were hired to create awareness. But what about when we're creating awareness and sending traffic to a website that is really bad at converting visitors? We have no control over the consideration phase of their marketing. Yet we're unfairly blamed for the lack of leads coming from our SEO work.

Successful leaders think holistically about their marketing strategy. For example, they don't believe that creating awareness through advertising automatically generates leads. They keep in mind that a marketing strategy must cover all three areas of the marketing funnel if it will be truly effective.

Remember to build experiences.

As leaders evaluate potential strategies, I encourage them to always think through the experience customers will have. Empathy is the most powerful skill set one can bring to creating successful online experiences for customers. In fact, this is so important for leaders to understand and embrace, we've dedicated an entire chapter to this topic.

Marketers can sometimes get carried away with too much enthusiasm built around the creativity in a strategy. I've seen more than my share of creative but irrelevant campaigns that went nowhere. Leaders need to be careful not to be lured into the vanity of looking smarter or more creative than other brands and losing sight of the user experience. It rarely works as effectively as it promises to. Instead, it's better to shift the focus to what the customer really needs or wants to feel and think, especially at the moment they are ready to buy. Empathy trumps creativity every time.

Consider the timeline.

In my experience, leaders seldom ask about the expected timeline for any given strategy. The expected wait time for returns on investments can vary radically from one strategy to the next, so it's important for leaders and their teams to have realistic expectations. For example, a content strategy will often take years before it gets momentum. A strategy built on paid visibility may see results in a few weeks or months.

Without a realistic timeline expectation, a leader cannot evaluate the success and the merits of a strategy. It's not uncommon for a strategic marketing plan to garner disappointing results at first. A leader has to understand whether to wait and give it more time, to adjust the execution, or to change strategies. Without understanding the timeline needed to give the strategy a fair chance, it will be difficult to make that determination. We'll discuss this important leadership topic in more detail later.

Should We Change Our Strategy?

Bonnie was an independent marketing director and represented several clients as an outsourced Chief Marketing Officer. She used my agency for the fulfillment of digital marketing contracts she helped to construct, and for monthly execution and reporting on online advertising for her accounts.

Bonnie loved to be in front of her clients and keep them excited about a plan. But in her enthusiasm for keeping things "exciting," she would frequently request time to talk about strategy with our team. Worse, she asked us to talk about strategy for the same clients month after month.

I found this particularly stressful until the day I realized Bonnie didn't really want to talk about strategy, she wanted to talk about new creative ideas for executing tactics. In fact, not only were her conversations not about strategy, she was rarely working off a true and guiding strategy for any of her clients. Bonnie was using the word *strategy* in place of the word ideas.

A smart business leader doesn't change strategies frequently. In my experience, a strategy should be reconsidered with about the same frequency as a business plan update. Some strategies are long-term, while others succeed or fail in a shorter time frame, but only fools change strategy monthly. Smart businesses experiment with tactics in service to a long-term, carefully thought-out strategy.

Some of the most important jobs of the leader are to understand and sign off on the overarching strategy, participate in its development, and make the call as to whether to stick with it or take a different approach in due time.

By asking their teams to articulate a simply stated strategy, even leaders without confidence in marketing will begin making an impact. By participating in strategy development and making sure the approach is holistic, addresses core problems, and implements unique opportunities, even an inexperienced leader can effectively guide this complicated aspect of their business growth.

CHAPTER SUMMARY

- Leaders must make sure their organizations are intentional about choosing and following an excellent marketing strategy.

- An excellent strategy can be described coherently, identifies the business's biggest challenges, and outlines a plan to overcome them.

- A good marketing strategy addresses the three phases of marketing: awareness, consideration, and decision.

- In marketing strategy development, businesses should first look at what is already working, how their customers are finding them, and what obstacles currently exist.

- Good strategies are often built around key, unique insights business leaders have about their own company, the market, and/or their clients.

- Leaders should have a realistic expectation for a strategy's timeline, then be careful not to change strategies too soon, or hold onto an unsuccessful one too long.

How Are We Different?

Dale and Roger: A Tale of Two Plumbers

Neither Roger nor Dale launched their businesses with any financial advantage. They both started out with their pickup trucks, magnetic signs on the doors, and ads in the local phone book. They grew their businesses one customer at a time. They were both proud of themselves and of each other, and sometimes reminisced about the tough years they had endured.

But eventually, Dale's success meant something different. It made Roger feel like he was somehow being outdone or left behind. What disturbed Roger most was that three years ago, he was out-pacing Dale in sales. Since that time, he had been out-spending Dale in advertising, yet falling behind. How had Dale gotten ahead? They had used the same advertising and marketing vendors, and Roger had a stellar sales team.

How was it possible that Dale was now growing his top line by 30 percent year-over-year for three years straight, while Roger struggled to grow by 5 percent? Their markets were nearly identical. Both companies were up against the same competition, a national plumbing and heating franchise, in their territories. How had Dale pulled ahead?

Even more perplexing, just four years earlier, Roger's sales were 20 percent ahead of Dale's. He was proud of the company he had built, and without intending to, Roger had used Dale's business as his benchmark. Every quarter, when they met and discussed their businesses, he felt good about his success seeing he was outpacing Dale. What had brought Dale out of his sales slump? What was driving this amazing growth? He had to know.

Roger was known for making smart, safe, and sensible decisions each step of the way. In fact, other businessmen came to him for counsel. Adding to this, he had a talented leadership team in place, and he always sought out wise advice from these trusted advisors. And that's what made this even more troubling to Roger. Dale tended to be more of a risk-taker and didn't always make good business decisions, by Roger's standards.

A few years ago, Dale decided to give up pursuing commercial and industrial clients in favor of serving residential clients, which Roger thought was a bad decision. Even worse, he was going after stay-at-home parents in nearby affluent neighborhoods. Dale's guiding insight was that 40 percent of his company's calls were from stay-at-home moms or dads who were dealing with home maintenance issues such as leaking pipes, clogged drains, and failing air conditioning units. Since they were home during the day, the task of selecting and meeting the service people was frustrating for these harried homeowners. Dale also understood his team was great at making this clientele very happy. Their careful attention to showing up on time and being especially tidy made Dale's customers fiercely loyal.

Dale's company had updated their website with new content and branding elements. Dale had made sure his marketing team was talking to his sales and service people so they knew exactly what issues to address on their YouTube channel. Roger was aware that Dale had been doing this but felt that some of it was just too casual and unprofessional. Secretly, he was a little embarrassed for Dale.

Dale had also revised his service model. He insisted his service team now wear super-clean white shoes and put plastic shoe coverings over them before entering a customer's home. Service techs were careful never to track dirt into a customer's home, and the white shoes became part of their branding ethos. Dale tended to hire polite and kind service people anyway, but he trained them to use a specific script when they arrived and when they left.

He had a mobile app built so his customers knew exactly when the service technician would arrive at their home. These stay-at-home clients had surprisingly busy schedules, running kids to sports, getting babies to take naps, getting groceries, attending social engagements, and addressing other family concerns. Dale's customers wanted to squeeze a lot into their days, and they hated the four-hour appointment window Dale's competitors made.

Dale's drivers would also call 15 minutes before arriving at the door so the customer wouldn't be surprised by the doorbell. Having raised kids of his own, Dale knew that nothing was more irritating than having someone ring the bell, making the dog bark and waking the baby.

Each service encounter began with the service tech asking, "Is this still a good time?" Dale found that customers always said, "Yes, of course," but really seemed to appreciate being shown that respect.

At the time, Roger had thought Dale was crazy for making these changes. "Don't you realize what rebranding will do to the commercial side of your business?" Roger had asked. "Look at all that revenue you're about to lose! You're going to alienate a lot of potential customers who will choose a competitor instead of you," he had warned. "Do the math, Dale! How can this be a smart move? Besides, that is the most difficult sector of clients to satisfy!"

While Dale was using a more narrowly-focused marketing message, Roger was expanding his business to include plumbing installation for new construction. Roger's vision was to open up possibilities for growth in a variety of sectors. But in the last three years, Roger's company was taking a beating from the competition. And, as a full-service plumbing and heating company that served many different markets, everyone was his competition. Roger was being dragged into brutal price wars. Advertising budgets were never quite enough to keep up. New competitors from neighboring areas were luring customers away at perimeter areas of his service territory. Roger's customer base seemed less loyal than ever. Every day seemed like a fight to keep what he already had, let alone to grow his marketing share. Even worse, his need to discount prices to stay competitive was hitting his profit margins hard. He was working much harder to make less money than he had three years ago.

Meanwhile, Dale's base of happy stay-at-home parents referred their friends, and Dale's competitors couldn't begin to lure customers away from him. In fact, some other plumbing and heating companies that didn't want to deal with these "difficult to please" customers referred them to Dale. It was like Dale had zero competition. He was the big fish in the small pond of stay-at-home parents.

Meanwhile, Roger was like a little fish in a big pond who had no real marketing platform on which to grow marketing share. Since he had no clear differentiation, everyone was his competition. He had to compete on price to get the interest of potential customers.

Narrowing the Market

While this story is completely fictional, it might as well be true. Business leaders are often confronted with the choice of whether or not to narrow their market. Narrowing your market opportunities seems counterintuitive. Why turn away customers who are within reach? Why make your potential market smaller? How can this be an advantage?

Every month, when I talk to business owners who want to grow their market share, I ask them a simple question: "Why would someone choose your business over your competition?" There are two types of answers—generic and specific. Based on that leader's response, I can predict whether or not we'll have great success handling their marketing.

I asked that question to a furniture retailer some years back. Why did he believe customers should shop at his store? "Because his sales staff was friendly and helpful," he told me. I gently broke it to him that we have dozens of furniture store clients, and they all have friendly and helpful staff. He'd have to do better than that. His answer was too generic.

After giving me a showroom tour, he flipped a chair upside down and showed me the way the pieces of wood were joined together. "This chair won't wobble, even when the owner's grand-children inherit it in 40 years." His excitement was genuine. Now we were getting somewhere. I was now understanding his specific market, buyers interested in heirloom furniture.

At that point, it became obvious to me his employees were having different conversations with customers than his competition's employees. He was positioned to attract buyers who weren't buying furniture to throw away in five years. His was legacy furniture—beautiful, traditional, and competitively priced. With that defining differentiation, he was setting up his marketing to be successful.

That distinction, once understood and recognized, informed all the content we wrote, the images we chose for his website, and the script and visuals we portrayed in his video campaigns. He defined how they were different, and we leaned into it. It's the leader's job to gain clarity about their organization's differentiation and make sure all marketing aligns and reinforces it.

Leaning In

I first heard the expression "leaning in" from Suzy Batiz, the developer of Poo-pourri, the handy spray you use in toilet water before you "drop the motherlode," as she refers to it. With a relatively small budget, Suzy produced a video featuring a proper young British woman talking about embarrassing bathroom smells. It went viral on YouTube and was on the most-watched video list for quite some time. Google's YouTube team used this as a case study and brought her to their New York office. It was there I heard her talk about the Poo-pourri marketing strategy.

Rather than explaining the science behind how this miracle spray prevents odors instead of masking them, she chose to use third-grade-level potty humor. As Suzy explained it, "We looked at ourselves and identified what was a little weird about our product, and then we leaned into it." Had Suzy marketed by simply talking about the product's features and benefits, it would have never become the viral sensation or gained such marketing traction. And that would stink.

That's exactly what you must do as a leader. You must be intentionally self-aware enough to clearly understand how your brand is different. As you direct your marketing, you need to be sure this differentiation informs everything your marketing stakeholders do.

Great leaders define a niche, and this creates a powerful platform for marketing to be exponentially more effective. Leaders who have the courage to be different can own a niche. That's why many smart marketers today will tell you it's better to be different than it is to be better. Leaders must champion differentiation, and make sure it is the right kind of differentiation, genuine, and meaningful to their clients.

Many business leaders believe outlining features and benefits is more effective when marketing to a broad audience. They think marketing is simply about creating awareness—running marketing campaigns, doing search engine optimization, and building a great website—but they're wrong.

Consumers are drowning in marketing messages. As a result, they tend to be unreceptive to advertisements that aren't relevant to their specific situation or need. Running general awareness campaigns that don't have specific relevance for a targeted audience will probably not get the traction you hope for.

Years ago, an environmental services company from New York City contacted me. They wanted me to help build a new website and develop an online marketing plan. With question after question, I couldn't get them to explain why someone would hire them over their competition. When it came down to creating content, they asked me to read their competitors' websites and basically rewrite that information for their own company. I'm not sure if they're still in business, but I can't find a trace of them online anymore.

Unless your business has some rare and sustainable barrier of entry, you will benefit in the long run by choosing to carefully and strategically differentiate your brand. It's nearly impossible to get traction for a brand when a company hasn't thought through their differentiation or their market position relative to their customers' other choices. It's a foundational element of business success. That's why great leaders ask themselves this very important question: *"How are we different?"*

Being Different

While it might seem simple to do, it takes tremendous courage and conviction for you, the leader, to narrow your market and define your brand's differentiation. Even your trusted advisers may become your adversaries in this. They may point out what you'll lose and how you'll be alienating existing market sectors. They'll remind you that your narrowed market is considerably smaller. Smaller market potential never feels right until you do the math. Ease of owning that smaller market share is always better than the unrealized potential of a large market. Comfort yourself with these words, maybe pop open a Red Bull, and keep reading.

How would you feel if you launched a new beverage only to face some scathing reviews about how unhealthy it was? That's exactly what happened to Red Bull. Consumer groups, concerned mothers, and health advocates stood united against this drink with its ridiculously high sugar and caffeine content. What did Red Bull do? They didn't waver. In fact, they leaned into their newly found bad reputation. I'm sure there were committees recommending they quickly develop a Red Bull Green with half the caffeine and nutritional value equivalent to one serving of kale. But that wasn't Red Bull's brand position. They did nothing to please concerned consumers. Surprising to many at the time, they actually embraced the bad press. It made their adrenaline-filled, living-on-the-edge, young audience identify more easily with this "bad-boy" drink. It worked.

Committees are notoriously bad at creating effective brand positions. When a leader delegates this responsibility to a committee, they are setting their business up for mediocrity. Putting a committee in charge may feel right to a leader. After all, they're getting buy-in. But committees tend to take decisions to a safe middle ground that makes everyone comfortable. Great brands don't please everyone. In fact, they ignore or even alienate some people who aren't their intended audience. To build a great brand, you have to be willing to say who your audience is and, by default, who it isn't. Are you ready to do that?

This type of brand positioning requires a courageous leader who understands the importance of differentiation and is willing to fight for it. If you're the type of leader who is addicted to having consensus before making a bold decision, you may find yourself in trouble directing your business's marketing. Great leaders don't allow committees to make these types of decisions.

Many leaders I've helped believe their brand is made up of their features and benefits. They want to use them as differentiating points. But these almost never differentiate a brand. When it comes down to features and benefits, companies look similar to customers. Brands need to take it a step further, like a cartoonist does when making a caricature.

For example, I once was discussing differentiation with a businessman who told me his company's uniqueness was in their honesty, caring, and dependability. I had to gently break it to him that his audience doesn't think of those attributes as special. They were expected. It was like a restaurant saying, "We serve food."

When a business talks about their features and benefits, they usually list features that are not as differentiated as they think. It's all about the consumer's impression, not that of the business-owner. Your brand must have a distinguishing position that truly stands out. Businesses typically believe they are more differentiated from their competition than the public's actual perception of them. Leaders should always keep in mind that the consumer ignores subtle differentiation. That's why effective marketing exaggerates it.

To make this even more problematic, consumers' attention spans are quite short. You need a brand position that strangers can easily understand and identify with. If you're starting with features and benefits as your differentiation, you need to take it up a level.

Consider Dale's business; his employees wore shoe coverings in order to keep their clients' homes clean. That was a feature of their service and a benefit to consumers, but their brand differentiation was "We're the right fit for stay-at-home parents, who typically don't want to clean up after a plumber."

Some business leaders don't have any vision for their own differentiation. Consequently, they believe they simply need to outspend their competition in creating awareness, and advertise more. But I'm convinced almost every company has an opportunity to amplify something slightly different about itself, thus creating a powerful strategic advantage over time.

Find Your Differentiation

When my customers get stuck, I take them through a simple exercise. First, I have them list everything they can think of that makes them different from their most similar competitor. I suggest they consider things like their personality, what they commonly hear customers say about them, how their customers are different, what their unique customers have in common, and how the experience they provide their customers is different. It's great to make this list as long as possible, adding lots and lots of adjectives and other sentences they can say about themselves that other similar companies can't.

Next, I ask them to start a list of things important to their customers. This can get confusing because there are really two types of attributes. There are the things that build first impressions, and there are things that make customers loyal. It's the first-impression attributes that will be most helpful in this exercise. Feedback from customers is helpful in creating this list, along with industry research and interviews with client-facing employees. Client-facing employees include people who answer phones, salespeople, and account managers. What do potential customers quickly see that attracts them to you or helps them identify with your product, service, personality, culture, or point of view "from a mile away"?

The third step in this exercise is where it all comes together. What showed up on both lists? What is unique to you and also valuable for attracting new customers? The intersection of these two lists is typically where you'll find the best ideas for your brand's differentiated position.

Sometimes it isn't obvious because the lists don't seem to intersect. For example, on your first list, you may have said your massage studio has "off-street parking and walk-in chair massages," but your other list may say, "convenient service." That's the same thing and may inspire you to position your spa as, "a massage exactly when you need it."

Many brands only work off of their first list. A few years ago, an appliance retailer approached my agency for marketing help. The owner and founder, now well past retirement age, insisted their brand position be built around the fact that they had been in business for more than 50 years.

I loved the fact that only they could say this and their competitors couldn't. It was great to see the pride the owner had in his brand. But their 50 years in business didn't matter much to their audience of potential appliance buyers.

May I Have Your Attention Please?

It's also important to remember how little of an audience's attention you have. You need a very simple and succinct message or idea, one that can easily communicate your unifying brand position. If you can't explain it in three words or fewer, you more than likely need to keep working on it.

Some brands make this too complicated and think about it too much, ending up with a message that is philosophical, even ethereal. Nothing is less helpful than meeting someone at a networking meeting and asking them what they do only to have them say, "We enrich lives." After another five painful minutes of questions and studying their business card, you discover that they install kitchen cabinets. "We enrich lives" may be a great internal message to inspire their team, but it's not a brand position and shouldn't be used as one.

Contrast that with a very successful local painting company in my area called Two Dudes Painting. Without any explanation, you probably already understand the company's ethos. Customers easily identify with and like their brand position, especially because the personality of the company is fun and approachable (and they do great work!).

Your job as a business leader is to be keenly aware of your differentiation and ensure that your stakeholders understand it. Keep in mind your brand is expressed in the total experience your customers and employees have with your business. You can't be the "friendly family bank" then send scathing first notices when a payment is late.

Southwest Airlines should get a lot of credit for doing this right. Part of their brand position is to be fun. Flying can be stressful and consumers like me enjoy the easygoing culture the airline portrays. The flight attendants' playfulness and witty remarks have made many of my business trips more pleasant and have made me a loyal fan.

Some leaders have a gut feeling about their differentiation but have never learned to communicate it succinctly. It reminds me of a very, very long email I sent to a coworker. I apologized for its length and concluded with: "If I had more time, I would have made this shorter." Succinctness is difficult and requires a lot of thought. You need to dig deep into the central unifying concept, word, ethos, kernel of insight, or even mantra that represents your brand differentiation, then create concise language that captures it and use it in all your marketing.

Remember, your differentiation will always be relative to your customers' other choices. When I want to ship a package, if it is really important to have it there on time, I choose FedEx. "On-time delivery" is the brand differentiation compared to other carriers in my mind and in the minds of consumers like me. That's why when you describe your brand differentiation to your stakeholders, you'll find yourself using language that is comparative. You'll say things like, "We're more dependable, more expensive, more affordable, faster, more thorough, more trustworthy, and more fun." If you are using comparative language, you're probably on the right track.

Create Your Niche

Often the best marketing opportunity for a brand is to further contrast itself with its competition. Consumers' minds have one mental category for plumbers. If you're the always-on-time plumber, you better make sure to amplify that so much that consumers make a new mental file for your company. You create a new niche in their minds. This makes you more memorable and builds a strong affinity with your intended niche audience.

If you don't work hard enough at this, bad things happen. Your customers will democratize your brand, making you so similar to your competitors, you'll have to compete mostly on price. If you don't demand to be different, your customers will define your brand position, and that's the worst position in which to put your company. Everyone in your industry becomes your competitor if you don't differentiate.

It's your job as a leader to ask and answer the question, "How are we different?" Branding experts can help you through this process, but ultimately, you must own this vision of differentiation and insist that all your company's activities align with it.

Being different is only as effective as your ability to communicate that differentiation to an audience with whom it resonates. Your marketing team's job (whether it's in-house or an outside agency) is to reach that audience and to clearly contrast your brand position from that of your competition. That's because your company's brand differentiation is only as real as the audience's perception of it. While you might decide to move into a specific market position (e.g., be the ideal local residential plumber), the audience must position you in the same way.

As the company's leader, you have to be sure your stakeholders follow two guiding principles: *clarity* and *consistency*. A good branding company can help you craft language and create visual clarity that best characterizes your brand position. Deputize yourself as "Captain Consistency."

Consistency means your brand is represented accurately at every touch point. If part of your brand is "friendly and supportive," you can't have a rude person answering the phone. If your brand is about being a "smart, reliable, expert writer," you can't have typos in your work. Ever.

Everything that your customer base experiences through you is part of your brand. As a leader, you need to make sure it is aligned, and that customers always experience the same thing every time, month after month. This is the part of your company's marketing you are most responsible for, and your leadership in this area will prove to be more powerful than you'll ever realize. Great leaders are persistent and tenacious.

The Journey Forward

It's important to be prepared for pushback when you decide to position your brand, especially if things are going well. Owning a niche may alienate potential customers. That's going to feel counterintuitive. I believe this is especially true for young businesses being run by their owner/founder, which applies to my situation.

I started YDOP, an internet marketing company, in 2006. At the time, being a digital agency in Lancaster, PA, and developing social media strategies and search engine optimization (SEO) for businesses was already an impressive differentiation that earned us fast growth.

I was fortunate to find some great mentorships with agencies on the west coast who were a few years ahead of us, successfully serving large national brands. I traveled there regularly and was able to ramp up quickly in the emerging digital marketing industry from that mentorship.

I quickly built a super-smart core team able to take on all sorts of complicated assignments. My core competency in business development combined with a smart team allowed us to quickly grow as a successful, start-up boutique agency. We were able to take on any assignment, and that's exactly what we did.

At the time, I thought our brain-power and ability to serve a variety of clients was our strength. But a few years later, it became obvious this was actually our weakness. We were doing different things for all different types of businesses and industries. It was wearing us out.

I couldn't hire new smart-enough people to jump in and help the alpha-nerd team we had developed. Our sales growth began to slow, which made us even more desperate to take on any project that came our way.

While we were once one of the only choices in town for quality digital marketing, our differentiated position was becoming democratized. A few years later, other traditional shops were using the same language on their websites and in their marketing and sales materials. Being a "full-service digital agency" was a bland, non-differentiated position in a now-crowded market.

Finding Our Niche

In the midst of this change, my lead strategist and I attended a digital marketing conference in Arizona. During a break, we met up to discuss what we had learned so far. He said, "I learned there are more than 20 different types of social media agencies in the United States. Which one are we?" His question made us both laugh, but it drove home a painful point. We were a boutique agency in an expanding industry. We needed to define a niche and put our stake in the ground.

Admittedly, making that determination wasn't easy, and it took longer than I would have liked. Looking back, three questions gave us the insights we needed to find our niche:

1. What are we really good at already?
2. In what direction is our industry headed?
3. What does the market want?

At the time, we had a few dozen clients, and a specific grouping were exceedingly happy with our work. They all had one thing in common: they were local service providers and local retailers. That's what we were good at, and that's what we could do better than anyone else.

Also, our industry was changing. Google was recognizing there was a significant amount of search activity with local intent. Local intent means that when someone searches for "pizza" on Google, they're looking for a pizza shop nearby, not a Wikipedia article on the history of pizza or a recipe. Google began showing a different search engine results page for queries with local intent. These results pages gave local businesses a significant opportunity to be found by nearby customers. Most business owners at the time weren't aware of the advantage Google was giving local businesses and this marketing opportunity. We had a chance to provide outstanding value to them.

One of our local retailers, a music store chain, gave me some incredible feedback. The owner said, "Steve, I believe your business is really going to take off, and here's why. Business owners like me know we should be using the internet, but we're just not sure how to do it well. We need a trusted partner like you to help us."

That was the insight and the confirmation I needed. Shortly after, we created our mission statement, "To be the ideal internet marketing partner for businesses with nearby clients." We registered and were awarded the trademark for Near-user Marketing® and put our stake in the ground as the first, and only, company in our area to be the best at serving businesses with localized markets.

Desperate Beginnings

I wish I could tell you we lived happily ever after, but it didn't go that way. Like most companies that narrow their markets, there is a price to pay. The year we made that decision was the only year in our 12-year history that our topline sales decreased from the previous year. It was scary. We dipped far into our credit line. I questioned my decision many times that year. Had I done the right thing?

If you are the business founder, narrowing your market and creating a niche is especially difficult. Why? Because you survived the first few years by not being narrow or selective. You did whatever you had to do to get business. Now you are going a different direction and in the short term, it could hurt profits and growth.

I remember driving to a dangerous part of The Bronx to meet a potential client. When we got there, we couldn't find the business using the address we were given. It turns out because we were in a black sedan, they thought we might be from the government, so they didn't answer when we knocked on their door. A phone call straightened out the misunderstanding. Then, several men dressed in black suits escorted us through the building and onto a fire escape, over to another building, and up three floors to the boss's beautiful (and well-hidden) office suite. I remember thinking, "Oh my. The things I do to get a client!" That feeling was amplified when they were brought up on murder charges a year later.

That willingness to run at any and every opportunity is often how businesses survive in the early years. But it is also what can keep a business from maturing, especially if the owner/founder never makes this transition. Leaders must mature past the years when they took any profit opportunity that knocked on their door.

I still remember sitting in my office talking to my business coach about how I probably made a bad decision having YDOP specialize in Near-user Marketing®. I stopped going after other types of clients and only concentrated on localized businesses. Our new brand position was starting to kick in, but the growth it created didn't outpace the losses we were seeing. It was killing me not to pursue opportunities that were high-paying, but out of our wheelhouse. That had always gotten us through in the past.

I felt like I was in an airplane heading toward the ground, pulling up on the yoke as hard as I could. Would we crash?

My coach wisely asked me, "Is this still a good idea?"

"Yes, I believe it is," I replied.

"Then you need to take heart and keep believing in it and fighting for it."

I am so grateful for his encouragement. The following year, we nearly doubled, and in four years, we had grown 400 percent. Our profit margins grew, too, as did our client retention and employee retention rates. What more could I have asked for?

Staying Different

Maintaining differentiation is an ongoing responsibility for any leader because differentiation evaporates. Even after establishing our niche brand of localized digital marketing, we soon saw its power eroding. I refer to it as *insidious brand democratization*. Little by little, you aren't so special any more. Competitors begin using your language on their websites and offering similar services. "Me-too's" pop up all around you, which makes you look less and less unique.

It is important to continually fight to position your brand with as much differentiation as possible. This is an ongoing responsibility for any successful leader. You can't expect your marketing department or agency to take on this responsibility, and if you have allowed your brand to lose its distinction over time, good marketing won't save it. The amount of money you'll need to spend and the discounts you'll need to give customers will make any gains disproportionate to what you'll spend on marketing.

Businesses that have come to us over the years with their niche figured out bring our marketing company the opportunity to do great work for them. We know exactly whom to reach and with what message, how to craft the perfect call to action, and the language needed to get that conversion. Businesses that come to us as "me-too" businesses need to work much harder and spend much more to get the same results.

Your marketing department/agency's job is to take your market position and get brand momentum, which should result in sales leads. It's not a marketer's job to invent who you are. It's your job to be able to articulate your differentiation to your stakeholders and make sure it is completely understood and consistently reinforced.

If you want to be a great leader and direct your marketing and business development efforts to their highest potential, develop the discipline of asking, "How are we different?" If you're like most business owners, finding the answer will be difficult because it's not how you're accustomed to thinking.

You don't need to become a marketer to do this, but you may need to hire one. Don't confuse a room full of graphic designers with a brilliant branding company. If you hire the right talent to help you through this process, they'll ask you the right questions and will help you craft language, symbols, fonts, colors, logos, and taglines you need to build a powerful brand.

Understanding clearly how you're different and having a vision for creating a brand around that distinction will empower you to hire the right marketing stakeholders, to enter into meaningful conversations with them, and to direct them to do their best work for you!

CHAPTER SUMMARY

- Narrowing a business's marketing focus may seem counterintuitive to a business leader, but there are many long-term rewards for doing it and risks in not specializing.

- Specializing takes courage and conviction and must come from the top down in an organization.

- A business should choose a singular, uncomplicated, differentiated position relative to the competition.

- That differentiation should lie in the intersection of two lists—the ways the business is different, and the aspects important to an audience.

- The choice to differentiate may have some short-term costs but will pay off in the long term.

- Maintaining differentiation is an ongoing concern for a leader.

QUESTION

What Do Our Customers Experience?

In the mid-1960s, my family had a television that got three channels. Well, two channels came in clearly and the third did, too, but only if my sister was willing to hold the antenna in a certain way.

Times were simpler then, and so was technology. I remember my Friday evening line-up when three of my favorite shows aired back-to-back. I'd organize my snack next to my favorite chair and enjoy a fun evening of entertainment. Now I realize how strange this was. We watched every commercial and didn't mind! That's what people did back then. It was normal.

Major brands, such as Coca-cola and Procter & Gamble, experienced incredible growth during this era. For every $1 they spent on marketing, they earned between a $1.70 and $2 return.

If a smart leader had run a business during that time, what would they have done? It's simple. They would have spent every dollar they could find and used it for advertising. And that's what happened. Advertisers increased their television marketing air time to approximately six hours of advertising in a 24-hour period.

But something happened in our home. Our next television had a significant new feature—a remote control. We no longer had to watch commercials. The remote control turned us into "channel surfers," opening the door for consumer resistance to advertising. It was the first in a series of technology disruptions that would add layers of complexity to marketing.

Cable television was next. Soon, viewers like me had dozens (and later hundreds) of viewing options, and on the radio, even more options than ever before were available. Channel surfing became the norm, as did avoiding anything but the most interesting viewing at any given moment. The technology industry reacted and developed DVR devices (TiVo was the first) that recorded your favorite shows for later viewing and allowed you to skip the commercials. Video stores popped up across the country to fulfill our desire to conveniently watch what we wanted, commercial-free, of course!

Later, as personal computers became mainstream, consumers were now viewing a different screen, with a mouse in hand instead of a TV remote. This was a big deal for marketers. Consumers were now in complete control of what they would see. Consumer behaviors no longer resembled mindless zombies being programmed to choose one brand over another. Audiences were not only blocking and avoiding advertising messages, they were now choosing information.

As modern consumers, we've been given more control over what we see. With each iteration of technology, we are becoming more difficult to reach and influence through mainstream media channels. We are less likely to trust marketing messages. And advertising dollars are bringing less and less return on investment. Today's consumers want to be in charge of discovering and forming an opinion about a brand. They want to control the experience.

Search engines have made us even more fiercely independent

consumers. We can now research anything. If we need a new car, we can find out volumes of information before setting foot on a dealership's lot. Finally, we're no longer subjected to awkward conversations and sales pitches from pushy sales staff, at least not until we're closer to reaching a decision.

Right now, the internet is paving the way for streaming media giants such as Netflix, Amazon Prime, and Hulu. Now, we are one click away from any movie we could possibly want to watch, for only a few dollars a month. Driving to the video store is a relic from a simpler time. As of 2017, only a dozen Blockbuster stores remained open in the United States. Their last two stores, both in Alaska, closed in July 2018.

Each technology advancement has taught consumers to embrace their independence. Before making any purchase decision, whether it's a new furnace for my home or the best place to buy tube socks, I look for information online. Don't you? I can get tips for how to get stains out of my bathroom sink and discover good games for my son's next birthday party. I can research the best product for waxing my car when I'm drowning in choices at the auto parts store.

The smartphone took my consumer independence to a new level. Today, I can do all the things consumers do whenever it crosses my mind, no matter where I am. While I'm waiting in line at the bank, I can research lunch spots near me, learn which of them are the most popular, and read their menus. I can get directions with live traffic conditions for my intended route. I can see the photos that others have taken of the restaurant's interior and of its food while reading their reviews. I can even make a reservation.

And I can learn what others think of my potential car wax purchase, thanks to the emergence of social media. Sources of infor- mation are no longer only coming exclusively from brands. Now, I can easily find out what others think.

Everyone's a Critic

The popularization of online consumer reviews on social websites began a frightening era for many brands. Companies were no longer in absolute control of their brand's message. Stories of bad service, cold coffee, dirty hotel rooms, and horrific airline experiences were influencing consumers' opinions.

Consumers are armed with smartphones loaded with apps to post online reviews, a camera to capture the cockroach in the corner of the hotel lobby, and a video camera to capture airline security employees dragging a passenger off a plane. With the popularization of social media, businesses discovered a new challenge in managing their brands.

The days of watching three channels and being programmed to hold certain brand preferences are gone. A population of fiercely independent, salesperson-resistant, impatient, and research-savvy people have replaced old-school "zombie consumers." A highway billboard will do little to change customers' minds anymore. Effective marketing today involves interacting with a consumer who wants to be in control of brand discovery.

Branding is Not Enough

Unless we understand that the people we want to reach are partly in control of discovering us, we will be tempted (as many leaders are) to take 1960s approaches. We'll spend a lot of money on media space for our commercials, which is expensive relative to its impact.

In the previous chapter, we discussed differentiation and, along with it, creating a brand position that helps a potential audience easily identify with that brand. This is a crucial platform for a business to build in order to be successful today. But it's not enough. Today's audiences have been and are being bombarded with more messages and advertisements on more channels than ever before. What are we going to do to stand out from the noise?

In the 1960s and '70s, the secret to success was advertising investment. The key was to find money in budgets for advertising, then manage the media spend effectively. But in the more crowded advertising era of the 1980s, it took more than effective budget management. Creativity became the new silver bullet. In January of 1984, Wendy's launched an advertising campaign featuring actress Clara Peller, who coined the phrase, "Where's the beef?" The ad was a creative and hilarious mockery of other fast food restaurants' comparatively small meat portions. This clever campaign is credited for boosting Wendy's' annual revenue by 31 percent that year.

Today, storytelling is a powerful and effective method companies are using in their marketing campaigns. The pro-storytelling argument is based on the idea that the human mind is a story processor, not a logic processor. To get a brand's messages to sink into modern consumers' minds, marketers are applying basic storytelling principles.

A Well-Crafted Brand Story:

- Clearly establishes a brand's mission, purpose, and core values.
- Draws audiences into a problem and then helps them find a solution.
- Offers people an experience that makes them feel good, not just a mundane product or service.
- Encourages people to engage in that experience.

Marketing approaches have come and gone over the last few decades. In every case, the first companies to implement them successfully earned great visibility and eventual imitation. Copycats quickly democratize approaches, making them far less effective. Remember when blogging was a novel thing?

What happens when everyone is storytelling? Stories still influence audiences, but storytelling as a unique marketing strategy is no longer as effective. When everyone is telling stories, only the best are heard. The rest become noise. Today, businesses need to do more than create brand exposure and hope they can figure out a way to stand out in a crowded space using (now common) enhancements like storytelling.

Stuck in the Past

I'm convinced many leaders are unknowingly caught up in using marketing approaches no longer relevant to our time. An employee for a higher education client of ours believed budget and media purchasing were the keys to their marketing success. At one point, he said, "What we really need to launch this online degree program is a large marketing budget and a comprehensive marketing plan." I thought to myself, "If it were only that easy." He was stuck in 1960s thinking.

In an industry as competitive as higher education, they couldn't afford to execute a comprehensive plan. What they needed was a strategy for reaching a highly targeted audience, a specific type of student that would be interested in their niche offering. They needed to construct a persuasive message for that audience. Just as important, they needed to design an online user experience, one that would influence website visitors to enroll in the new online program.

Other leaders are stuck in 1980s thinking. They bring creative ideas for our video team to execute with the belief that it will elevate their brand and somehow grow their business. Owners love when a marketing agency or video shop produces a creative video that makes the brand look good. But unless it is a one-in-a-million production, is that really going to make an impact? Is that what consumers are really looking for?

Years back, restaurants were notorious for making this mistake. At the time, I was serving a client who wanted to reach several hundred restaurants in a specific area. He wanted a really artistic website that would be as impressive as we could possibly make it. I gave him pushback, saying this isn't really what his customers would like. He disagreed.

Weeks later, after he had looked through at least 200 restaurant websites, he knew exactly what I meant. One after another, most sites played music and then allowed visitors to click to enter. He had to listen to music, see special effects, and endure other things that restaurant-owners like him believed would impress visitors. In reality, restaurant website visitors like him want to see the menu, get directions, and make a reservation. Sure, the website should look professional and have great photographs, but visitors are there for a purpose and prefer a website that helps them carry out that purpose easily.

Focusing on being creative can produce results that are coun-terproductive for providing a good experience on a website, a mistake that often irritates or confuses audiences more than it impresses them. This is especially true when it affects the user's ability to easily complete a task or get the information they're seeking. When marketers go too far, they hurt the brand.

While it's obvious boring is bad in any marketing content, simply being creative isn't going to succeed as a core strategy either. Even the Wendy's commercial, if it were airing for the first time today, probably wouldn't get great results because there are so many other creative and entertaining advertisements vying for our attention. Frankly, using creativity as a primary marketing strategy is a dated approach. When brands try to make it a contest by being more creative, they run the risk of creating content which is irrelevant to their brand and marketing mission. As company leaders, we must always understand the times, the season we are in, and where our consumers are heading. If we are able to do this, we'll have a great advantage over our competition.

For example, as I write this chapter, a majority of internet searches are taking place on mobile devices. But if I'm in a room full of business owners and ask them to picture an excellent website in their minds that will be helpful to their audiences, no one reports picturing one in mobile size. Nearly all business leaders are still thinking about creating websites for desktop computers, while a majority of their audiences have moved to mobile devices.

That's why the key to good marketing in this generation is having intensely practical empathy. Empathy trumps creativity in an era where marketing is largely about creating user experiences. A good business leader works to understand how a market audience feels and what type of experiences they want to have.

Beyond Branding

In the last decade, I've met hundreds of business owners who didn't know how to grow their businesses or influence people to become customers. They advertise, pay for sponsorships, and buy media exposure. But most of that money seems to disappear without making a significant, measurable impact.

Businesses that focus solely on branding strategies struggle to build a solid business development model. In years past and today, businesses and organizations hired marketing companies to help with branding. That meant creating well-defined, consistent, and differentiated ways of representing their businesses. It encompassed visual elements like their colors, shapes, symbols, and of course, their logo. It defined things like their personality, culture, and genre. It may have included the language they used when talking about their brand, their services, and/or their products. It was a style guide to how they looked, how they sounded, and how they acted. "Brands build trust" was the mantra.

Once a brand was well-defined, marketing agencies helped with media purchases. That involved paying for media placement, increasing exposure of the brand to targeted audiences. The more brand exposures purchased, the more companies could expect to lure customers away from competitors. Today, however, market research shows that bought media exposure is less than half as effective as it was a few decades ago, yet it has become more expensive.

Many business leaders are constantly asking, "Where should I advertise to make the phone ring, email ding, or door swing?" But is that the key question to ask? If a leader isn't first asking their marketing stakeholders about customer experiences, they might not be ready to create more awareness.

Joe Needs a Wife

Joe was single and relatively happy, but he wanted to be married. His well-meaning friends at work were doing their best to help him.

Pete, who runs the business development division, told Joe, "It's a numbers game. You need to get out there and meet more women." That made a lot of sense to Joe, so he set a personal goal to meet a hundred women that weekend.

Then Larry from sales weighed in. "Joe, you need to talk about your unique features and benefits. Remember that people don't buy mattresses, they buy a good night's sleep."

Joe found this fascinating. So he thought through his features and benefits and practiced his short pitch in front of the mirror. That weekend, Joe met a hundred women and explained his unique benefits, then he proposed to each woman.

That didn't go so well. One woman even slapped Joe before she stormed off. Joe was discouraged when he returned to work Monday morning. But then the light bulb came on in Joe's mind. "I never consulted with Mark from the marketing team!"

Standing in the marketing department, Joe told his story. "I met a hundred women this weekend and asked them to marry me, but they all said 'no.' What's the problem?"

They all stood silent, thinking, then Mark said, "You need a new suit!"

Every frustrated business owner whose marketing company suggested a new logo to grow their business can relate to this story. But if their businesses are hurting, they aren't laughing about the overemphasis many marketers still place on selling "new suits" or sole reliance on a branding strategy in our digital era. Branding still matters, but it doesn't get Joe to the altar. Likewise, it's not going to drop enough profit to the bottom line to justify the marketing investment.

Today, some businesses are quietly succeeding exponentially more than their competitors. I've had the great privilege to see first-hand how these businesses find success. But unfortunately, they're the exception to the rule. Most businesses are still trying to buy brand exposure as a way to grow a business, and it's not working that well. The world has changed. If we're going to succeed in marketing a business, branding is typically not a stand-alone strategy, especially for a small business. It simply won't convert enough people into paying customers to justify the expense.

Joe was advised to get a new suit. He should have been told how to get the next date and other practical advice on advancing a relationship into a deeper commitment. He could have been told to focus on being romantic, being a good conversationalist, taking an interest in things she cares about, and ultimately, how and when to propose marriage. He'd buy her flowers or take her to an expensive restaurant at just the right time in the courtship. He'd create amazing experiences for her based on a deep understanding of how she feels. That empathy would inform Joe as to what experiences he'd need to create to move the relationship forward.

That's a lot like marketing is today. In digital marketing terms, those dates are user experiences like reading a blog post, getting helpful emails, reading positive reviews, watching an interesting video, or listening to an engaging podcast. In dating, there are small events, like having her return a text, and there are big events, like her agreeing to meet Joe's parents, or the two of them verbally expressing their love for one another. They are significant relation-ship milestones. In marketing, we call them conversions. They are things like filling out a web form, clicking for directions to the restaurant, subscribing to the newsletter, or calling the business.

A micro conversion might be a website visitor signing up for an email newsletter. It's great that a visitor did this, but it isn't as good as a macro conversion, like the customer calling to request lawn care services or clicking to schedule a consultation with a financial advisor. These macro conversions have a higher correlation to a customer's positive purchase decision than micro conversions.

Focusing on the Customer's Experiences

A leader needs to direct marketing with the same mindset that a successful entrepreneur uses to manage a restaurant. He or she is constantly noticing what sort of experience diners are having. Are their glasses full? Was their food properly prepared? Is the room temperature acceptable? Is the music right? Is the lighting right? Are the servers being attentive? It's all about keeping a thumb on the pulse of the user's experience. That's precisely the approach good leaders take to directing their marketing.

For example, before a business produces a successful online video, they'll have a number of new questions to ask. Rather than just focusing on the creative story and the production, they'll need to ask:

- How will people find this video online?

- If they do find the video, why would they click on it?

- Why would they watch the entire clip?

- What should we want them to do after the video is over—go to a website, subscribe to a YouTube channel, or watch the next video in a series?

In an opt-in world, we have to ask very different questions to get the answers we need to make effective marketing decisions. It's all about creating user experiences.

Effective leaders today understand how they want their brand to be positioned, as we discussed earlier, but they also understand that this starts with having up-to-date clarity on what their independent-minded consumers need to experience.

How many people didn't buy a product or call about services

because of negative things they read on a third-party website? How many people thought a company was second-rate because their six-year-old, poorly-maintained website loaded slowly? How many businesses lost potential customers because Google ranked a competitor higher on a search engine results page or because another company's website did a better job of hooking their customer?

As company leaders, we need to be asking the question, "What do our customers experience?" If you own a plumbing business and a potential customer is researching water heaters, will your brand be the one that provides answers to their questions on YouTube? Will they find your website if they are searching for plumbers within your service area? What will they read if they find online reviews for your business? Will customers discover your product pictures on Google's image search, or your competitors'?

A few months back, I had lunch with a colleague who runs a successful marketing firm. When I asked about the overarching strategy his team executes best, his reply was clear: "We help a business clarify and elevate their brand."

His team members were masters at taking a business through the process of understanding and communicating their differentiation. When I searched for one of their local retailers online, I couldn't find them. This is not a new business either. This is an established local retailer. Sure, this marketing company was elevating a brand on traditional media channels like billboards and magazines, but what good is it if no one can find the business when they're actually interested in purchasing? They were so brand-focused that they overlooked the most basic experience they needed to provide to customers: being able to find them!

This colleague, like many marketers, is stuck in executing outdated strategies. While they may say they have an integrated approach, mixing both traditional and digital approaches, they treat the internet as additional platforms for advertising, forgetting that the web is an interactive platform.

They rationalize that if the internet is where people are spending their time now, then that's where we need to interrupt them. The internet to them is a place to purchase additional brand exposure. This was especially evident when Facebook and Twitter were emerging. Brands saw this as a golden opportunity for free advertising. They created pages, hired interns to post content, and created content calendars for telling audiences all about their business.

It fell flat.

Facebook users didn't want brands acting like brands. Companies had to quickly pivot and shift from being public relations soundbite pushers to behaving like real human beings who were authentic, interesting, and helpful.

Small and medium-sized businesses typically won't experience great success simply by branding and media purchasing efforts. They simply will not see a return on the investment and sadly won't be able to measure the loss. Worse, their stakeholders may get caught up in the vanity of seeing their brand elevated. It's an ego rush to see a logo and advertisement on that billboard, in that TV commercial, or on that glossy magazine page. But what is it bringing to the top line? What is it doing to the bottom line?

This difference of thought came out in a recent phone call involving my digital agency's team, a branding company, and our shared client. The furious client, a local retailer, initiated the call. Their business had completely disappeared from Google's search results. The branding company had just done a site redesign, omitting most of the website's page content that my agency had created to answer visitors' questions. The branding company thought their new website was wonderful and impressive because it was artistic and used a minimalistic design. They even took the phone number off the homepage. We thought it was the prettiest website no one would ever find or want to use. The client agreed with us.

Consumers are impressed with a beautiful brand. But in the end, they also care about their experience. Can they easily understand and navigate a decision on the website? Is their experience helping them to take the next step? Metaphorically, brands love to build fancy red sports cars because they believe it will impress potential customers. What people actually want, and respond more positively to, is a practical family minivan—an experience that is helpful, practical, and gets them where they want to go with ease. For example, having the phone number on the homepage, easy-to-find directions, and current sale inventory beats having an impressive, minimalistic website that web visitors and Google's search engine hate.

As business leaders, we need to keep our radar focused on the user experience. Looking good will only get us part way there. We must put the ever-important question in front of our marketing stakeholders: "What are our audiences experiencing?" And with that, "What do our audiences need to be experiencing?" The ongoing consideration of these important questions will direct marketing stakeholders to focus on the right things and to make changes that will have a significant impact on marketing outcomes.

CHAPTER SUMMARY

- Changes in technology have given rise to changes in consumer attitudes toward brands and receptiveness to their influence.

- Consumers are less influenced by traditional advertising today than decades earlier.

- Consumers are fiercely independent, wanting to be in charge of discovering and researching purchase decisions.

- Leaders must recognize these challenges and prioritize interactive marketing. This involves creating the right experiences for consumers even before they've identified them themselves.

What's Our Marketing Problem?

A typical scenario played out in my conference room a few years ago when a local business coach asked me, "Should I use Facebook for my business?" My answer surprised him. I responded by asking him, "What's your problem?"

After an awkward moment, I went on to explore what he wanted to accomplish with his business in the near term, and what he saw as the issue that was getting in the way. We quickly uncovered that clearly, Facebook was not the solution. Sadly, the popular advice that leaders have available would have steered this businessman into setting up a profile or page on Facebook, a platform he was ill-equipped to use, and a tactic that had little to no alignment with his short-term strategy or business goals.

As business leaders are asking tactical questions, I often take them to a higher, strategic level of thinking. I change the question to, "What problem do we need to solve?"

It's a sad but common scenario—businesses spend valuable financial and time resources engaging in marketing exercises that aren't going to help. Meanwhile, they fail to identify their key marketing problem or problems, which if solved, will have a profoundly positive effect.

This way of thinking can be difficult, especially if a leader hasn't had a lot of experience in developing marketing plans. Let's examine this approach of identifying problems using a short story about a business owner named Randy and his coach, Mike.

Death By Marketing - Part I

Randy's lifetime ambition was to own and manage his own lawn care company. By all appearances, he was living that dream. He had three trucks on the road, two employees, and a part-time secretary. But after eight years, Randy had hit a wall. Sales were flat, profits were down, and Randy was frustrated and discouraged. Randy knew if he didn't make a change, his business would be facing financial ruin.

Randy built this company with his intense work ethic and the ability to network and sell his services. But as the company grew, he reached the point where he was too busy managing operations to work on new business development. Meanwhile, his kids' school activities and other family priorities began competing for his time as they grew older. He couldn't work those 75-hour weeks anymore doing networking and business development activities and needed to find a way to get new business that didn't require so much of his time. He needed to generate new business leads without doing all the work himself.

On the advice of a successful local marketing company, Randy tried investing in advertising to achieve that objective. He realized he had outgrown his early ways of business development that depended on him attending networking events. His plan was to substitute his personal presence in the community with a polished brand presence. But eighteen months later, Randy was feeling demoralized. His plan and his marketing investment hadn't paid off, and now he was cash-strapped. At the same time, he knew adding business development to his responsibilities again wasn't the answer. He just couldn't see himself going back to working those long hours again. That would be a real hardship for his family and not the best long-term solution for his company.

Financially, Randy would have to make a decision soon. Cash was tight due to investments he had made in marketing and the discounts he was offering to get new business. Randy thought his increased advertising spend would be offset within the same fiscal year by a projected increase in new business, but that didn't happen.

His company had been on several highly-visible billboards and on several radio stations during rush hour. On the advice of his advertising agency, he had run ads in the newspaper on a regular basis. When that new business didn't materialize as planned, Randy was left with the agonizing question, "What went wrong?"

All this was running through his mind as he drove into Mike's parking lot. Mike was one of Randy's commercial clients and a respected business consultant and marketing coach. Mike had sensed Randy was struggling and agreed to give him a free hour of consultation in exchange for some landscaping services.

"I'm really frustrated about my business this year," Randy said as he was still shaking Mike's hand, wasting no time. He handed Mike a copy of his marketing expenses. "I've tried to invest in my business to create growth. I did everything right. But it's just not working like I expected. I feel like I just burned through a lot of cash I'll never see again."

"I've had to stop all my campaigns," Randy said in a softer voice so Mike's secretary wouldn't hear it. "Cash is tight, and I'm worried about my business's future."

Mike and Randy headed into the conference room. Seated across the table from one another, Mike leaned forward slightly and asked, "Do you mind if I ask you a few questions?"

"Sure," Randy said.

"Your marketing report shows you've reached 40,000 locals with your message. From what I can see, it's a clear message that sets you apart as an affordable solution for the middle-class home-owner. Judging from your business's early growth and the success of your competitors, this seems like a good niche," Mike said. "So, who are these 40,000 people? Can you tell me the name of any of them? If you wanted to email them today to talk about a new lawn treatment solution, could you do that?"

Randy sat frozen, staring back at Mike, but this time, Mike didn't look down. "You've spent the bank on introducing people to your brand and helping them understand it. But you had no plan in place for helping those acquaintances become contacts!"

"When I give seminars on business development, I use the analogy of crossing a stream," Mike said, leaning back in his chair and pointing to a beautiful photograph on the wall above the table. It was a shallow river dividing two grassy fields, and it had several stepping stones for hikers to use for crossing it.

"Picture a large group of people standing on this side of the river. They represent potential customers who have never heard of you. On the other side of the stream are customers who all love you. They're your raving fans. In between are the stepping stones used to cross the stream. Those stones represent the stages of business development. It looks to me like you've only worked on one stone," Mike explained.

Randy sat spellbound at Mike's explanation. Mike continued, "When you advertised, you made them aware of you. They stepped off the bank onto the first stone that we'll call, 'Acquaintances.' And that's where you left them standing. Your marketing budget only paid for the first part of their journey across the stream."

Almost before Mike finished his sentence, Randy asked, "What's the second stone?"

"Good question," Mike replied. "It's 'Contacts.' Some people might refer to them as 'Connections.' When you're investing in creating awareness, you need a plan to convert those soon-to-be Acquaintances into Connections."

Randy looked confused, so Mike continued. "It seems to me your marketing investment likely made a lot of people aware of you, but you don't know who they are. You created acquaintances, but not connections. A better plan might have been to use that advertising to encourage your audience to use a coupon that would allow you to track how they heard of you, and to collect their information for follow-up. You could have driven them to a web page where they could sign up for emails or to connect on social media to get special offers."

"But I did have my website URL on every ad," Randy argued.

"Yes, but your website is basically a brochure, not a conversion tool," Mike explained.

That stung, but Randy knew Mike was right. He had saved money a few years back and made the website with help from his nephew, a website developer. Honestly, he was proud of it partly because he had helped build it, and he got a fair number of compliments on it from family and friends. But Randy didn't see it as something to invest in and he hadn't kept it updated. It rarely got him leads.

"I know I haven't put a lot of effort into my website," Randy confessed.

"Why is that?" Mike asked.

"Well, frankly, it's just not how we get business. I know my industry pretty well at this point, and honestly, it's not where my leads come from," Randy explained.

"I'm not surprised," Mike said. "Your site isn't really designed to give you leads. It's difficult to even find it, and when you *do* find it, well…"

"Well, what?" Randy asked intently.

"It makes you look inferior to your competition who I strongly suspect are indeed getting leads from their websites. Frankly, Randy, yours doesn't build confidence or help your customers follow up with you. It's not really laid out to convince people to connect with you," Mike said somewhat softly, as if to lessen the harshness of his criticism.

"Well, I really appreciate your honesty, Mike. I needed to hear this, I guess," Randy said.

"But the good news is that these are all things you can change," Mike said reassuringly. "Let me change the subject for a second and ask you a different question. Where do your leads come from?"

"My leads come from word-of-mouth, from referrals, and from my personal networking," Randy responded.

"Of course they do," Mike said. "That's how every good business gets leads. But how many of those people checked out your website before they called you?"

Randy paused to think about that. It's not something that ever really crossed his mind. "I'm pretty sure that a lot of them probably visit my website before calling," he confessed.

"Exactly!" Mike retorted. "And they hired you in spite of your website. Now think about how many more people have visited your website and never reached out to you."

"But we have our phone number right on the homepage with a large font that says, 'Call Now.' Is that what you mean?" Randy asked.

"Well, not really. Websites don't really work like the phone book," Mike explained. "In many cases, people today want to feel comfortable before they call. Most customers today resist calling unless they're a 'warm lead.'"

"What do you mean by a 'warm lead?'" Randy asked.

"When you meet someone at a networking event, and they check out your website and call you, they're a warm lead. They've met you, and they also know others who know you. A referral that comes from a friend is also a warm lead. But when a stranger sees your ad and visits your website, your website has to 'warm them up.' They are learning about you with very little basis for trusting you," Mike explained.

After a long, thoughtful pause, Randy asked, "How do I do that? How do I warm up a stranger who visits my website after seeing my ad?"

"I have to admit," Mike said, "this is the hardest part of marketing. Today, customers are fiercely independent and often don't want to call a business early in the decision process. More and more customers today prefer to connect with a brand in a non-committal way first."

"You mean like signing up for an email newsletter?" Randy asked.

"Yes, that's a great example, but even that is difficult today. Customers are reluctant to give up their anonymity. It's important to give them a good reason to do so…" Mike explained.

"Like?" Randy asked.

"…like explaining special offers or benefits your email subscribers or social media followers will get, or offering a free consultation if they fill out your web form," Mike said. "You need to offer something of value, and you need to make them comfortable. For example, try saying 'We won't send you a lot of emails,' or 'You can unsubscribe any time.' You can even experiment on your website and see which messages tend to work best over time."

"Okay, I think I get it. As I create awareness with my marketing, I should give them an easy next step where I'll have the opportunity to know who they are. I can't expect people to learn that I exist, then pick up the phone and call me," Randy said.

"Exactly!" Mike said, gently slapping his hand on the table for emphasis. "That may have worked years ago, but today's customers are fiercely independent. You need to think of winning business as a process."

"Is that true for every business?" Randy asked.

Mike smiled, pleased that Randy had asked such an insightful question. "To a certain extent, but not entirely." He paused to laugh at his own ambiguity and the face Randy was making. "Let me explain! Some industries by their nature have much more complex sales processes, while others are straightforward and transactional. When a consumer's decision involves a higher dollar amount, has high stakes, isn't easily reversed, or is one that a consumer isn't used to making, it becomes more complex—like hiring someone to handle your retirement, installing a pool in your backyard, or hiring someone to build a home. You don't do these things with a 'Buy Now' button on a website after seeing an advertisement."

"Okay, I think I'm following you, but where does that leave us in your stream?" Randy asked, pointing over Mike's head to the picture.

"Great question," Mike replied. "And that's the beauty of the 'Connections' stone. The thing about the digital age is that we're able to communicate easily with a lot of connections through email, retargeting them with display ads, with search engines, and on social media! You need to think of your contacts like airplanes. They're people who are on your radar, but who haven't 'landed' yet as customers. You need a plan for staying in touch with them and staying front-of-mind while they are circling the airport, so to speak. You need to make sure that when they're ready, they'll choose your company."

Mike could tell by Randy's posture his lesson was sinking in, so he continued. "And the next stone is the 'Customer' stone. You need to understand what it will take for your contacts to become customers."

"Sooo…" Randy paused to give himself time to organize his thoughts, "I need to figure out how to build connections that are my business prospects, and I need to figure out a conversion strategy for turning my prospects into customers?"

"I think you've got it!" Mike said affirmingly. "You need to be thinking about what your prospects need so they can make the decision. Customers get stuck, and you need to help them get unstuck."

Mike stood up, walked to his office window, and pointed to the school playground across the street. "Do you see those kids going down that slide?"

"Yeah," Randy replied.

Pointing at the playground slide, Mike continued. "That's what your website should be like for your visitors. If a prospect visits your website, they should just slide right into the next step, whether that means to schedule a free consultation, connecting with you on social media, or even calling to set up a time to meet. Sometimes you need to give them a comparison chart to position your offerings and prices against the competition. That way they don't get hung up with the feeling that they haven't done enough research. Testimonials and reviews are a great help, especially if they are verified on other websites you don't control. Sometimes it's important to give website visitors more details about a next step. For example, instead of saying 'Call now,' say 'Call to speak with Sharon about our Weed-Free Guarantee program we're offering in your area.' Overall, it's about helping them take the next steps and removing any friction."

Just as Mike said this, he and Randy watched a young boy shoot down the playground slide so fast he couldn't get his feet on the ground at the bottom, sending him off the slide in a seated position. "I guess that's the way my website is supposed to work," Randy said, grinning.

Randy's countenance had completely changed. He had a new-found structure for thinking about his marketing, and he was ready to diagnose his marketing problem at a high level both now and in the future by asking a key question, "What's our marketing problem?" In other words, do more people need to hear about the product or service? Do we need to be better at building and staying in touch with potential customers? Do we need to make it easier for customers to take the next step on our website? And which key areas of our marketing should be improved?

Playing Dominos

Most children are fascinated with setting up rows of dominos, tipping the first one, and seeing them all fall in succession. This is a perfect analogy for the requirements of marketing today. The first domino might represent the initial experience of a person discovering your brand, and the last, the final thing marketing is responsible for. That might mean having that customer arrive at your store, send you an email, or call.

For years, marketing was made up of two dominos, the first and the last. The first domino was exposure. The last was the sale. Salespeople filled in the gap. Before they were warm leads, customers had to contact brands, request brochures, or visit business locations to get more information. This gave salespeople the opportunity to make contact, to divulge information, and to then follow up with the customer.

Today, business owners frequently tell us they "just want people to call" because their salespeople have such a high rate of converting callers. For the most part, this is a naive objective because customers are increasingly resistant to calling until they are a warm lead.

Meanwhile, salespeople may feel they are rock star performers today. They fail to consider that, compared to 20 years ago, the calls they get today are from customers who are already a lot further along in their purchase decision process. Many are already very warm leads before they even speak to the salesperson.

Years back, the role of a marketing agency was to work hard on that first domino. They would buy media exposure in their clients' target markets. They would keep tipping over that first domino until eventually it caused the second domino to fall. Many refer to this practice as "creating brand exposures." Extensive market research has been done over the years to answer the ever-elusive question, "How many brand exposures does it take to influence an individual's buying decision?" When I'm in the grocery store aisle deciding between two brands of soup, which one will I buy? My prior marketing exposures certainly have an influence.

Advertising, or buying brand exposure, still works but is not nearly as effective as in years past. Various hacks have and will continue to become popular and will eventually fade out again. Being creative, using sexuality and stunning minimalistic design, and storytelling are just a few approaches branding companies have used to stand out in the crowded advertising space, but even these become ineffective as copycats follow suit. Businesses like Randy's can spend a fortune on such tactics and see little return.

The strategy of brand elevation as a stand-alone approach is not going to work today for a great majority of businesses. Customers are fiercely independent and aren't so easily persuaded, even if you manage to capture their attention in a crowded marketing space. Even so, most business leaders like Randy are easily persuaded to spend an unreasonable amount of their marketing budgets for first domino experiences. Like Randy in our story, they believe exposure alone is the key to growth. Today, that rarely works, especially for smaller businesses.

As a business leader, you're going to be faced with the temptation to buy that billboard space along the highway or that radio time during the morning commute. Seeing your brand in the limelight can be enticing, and it's easy for brands to follow their egos into overspending on market exposure. But will you see the necessary return on that investment?

Clearly, there are more options to reach potential customers today than ever. That's especially true because of the internet.

What's Your Problem?

A friend named Barry came to me with the challenge of growing his business. He asked me straight away, "Should I start blogging?"

"That depends," I replied. "Is your problem that not enough people know about your business? Do people have trouble under-standing what you do and why they should hire you? Do you have a strong list of connections with whom you are staying in touch? Do your connections typically become clients, and do you know why or why not? Are your happy customers referring new business, and have you set up any systems or mechanisms to encourage or facilitate that?"

Barry had read some articles about how businesses like his should be producing content, and that every business should be blogging. When he talked to an agency that helps businesses do that, they agreed. But Barry knew it was a big commitment, and he wasn't confident he'd be able to keep up. I reminded him that a blog can be an important part of a marketing strategy, but there are many businesses like his that are wildly successful without one.

Many business leaders are tempted to feel a sense of loss because they aren't keeping up with every new thing. Their competitors are blogging and making videos, but they aren't. I typically remind them a good strategy will out-perform a shotgun approach that tries to implement every marketing tactic. This is especially true for smaller businesses.

But a leader can't truly discern which marketing strategy to run with until they've taken the time to look at the big picture. What is keeping people from becoming customers? What area of the stream do we need to work on most? Do enough people know about the business? Are bad reviews hurting us? Do our competitors look just like us but with lower prices? Is our web presence dated or ineffective?

Typically, leaders are too quick to believe their biggest problem is not enough people are hearing about their company, that they need to advertise more. They may even be making a bad impression with poor quality advertising, but they still want to make up for it with volume.

Consider this question: "If a potential customer heard of you, but didn't give you their business, what most likely happened? What stopped them from hiring you or buying from you?"

Whether you know it or not, at least some people are finding out about you and researching you online. Before you spend money on creating awareness for your business, you should find out the answer to this question: "If someone checks you out online, visits your website, and doesn't take any action, what happened? Assuming they were the type of customer you were hoping to get, what stopped them? How did you fail to give them the experience they needed?"

Helping Customers Say "Yes"

While it's going to be different for every industry, here are a few guidelines that will help remove friction from the customer's buying decision. The content you place on your website, which includes images and videos, should help the customer subconsciously feel these things:

1. They have what I want or need.
2. They are a good fit for me.
3. They're my best choice.
4. I feel comfortable taking the next step.

They have what I want or need.

If you've ever spent time on the web, you've more than likely come across a website that even after looking at it for five minutes, still doesn't explain what the company does. It's maddening.

It's important to build your company's homepage in a way that communicates what your business does in the simplest way possible. If you're a plumber, say so. Don't say "We improve the quality of life for homeowners" paired with a stock photo of a smiling family and a Golden Retriever sitting on a lawn, having a picnic. Rather, say something like, "Plumbing services for homeowners in Lancaster and York counties."

They are a good fit for me.

I remember walking through the mall with my wife when she was shopping for a new dress. We were in front of a store that seemed to me like it had a lot of nice clothes, so I suggested we go in. "No," she said. "That's not my kind of store." To this day, I'm still not sure why it wasn't. But somehow, she had positioned it categorically as a store that didn't have what she was looking for. Just like my wife made a categorical judgment, consumers across the board do the same.

As a business leader, it's important to remember people aren't necessarily making logical decisions about choosing your business over their other options. That's one reason why leading with the facts about "how you're better" doesn't work well most of the time. That's also why it's crucial to have already asked and answered the question, "How are we different?" With the answer in place, you can make sure that your intended audience can recognize that you're the right fit for them. You need to make all your written content, images, tone, and every brand representation resonate with your audience. You want your audience to say, "They are a good fit for me."

They're my best choice.

There is a common reason why people decide not to choose your company. When it comes down to the wire, the question, "What are my other options?" runs through their minds. Customers often don't feel comfortable enough to move forward and call you, email you, sign the deal, buy the product, sign up for the service, or press the "Buy Now" button if there are lingering concerns. "Is there a better option out there? Can I get this cheaper somewhere else?" They fear future regrets, those self-punishing thoughts about having made a bad decision.

But rest assured, there are several ways to address this. Some companies use comparative charts that show how they compare to similar offerings from competitors. It's important not to discredit competitive options. Simply position your company's offerings to show you're the right fit for your audience. Keep in mind you don't have to be the cheapest to be the right fit. For example, you might demonstrate yours is the only product that comes with a lifetime warranty.

Using trust symbols in your marketing is also helpful. If you're a member of the local Chamber of Commerce, the Better Business Bureau, or have certifications or member affiliations with organizations your audience recognizes, use them on your website. Some conversion scientists recommend having these symbols in proximity to "call-to-action" buttons on your website, like the "Send" button on a contact form. Guarantees are also helpful in calming these fears. Let people know if they move forward, there are options available to reverse their decisions.

When presented in the right way, testimonials are also very powerful. At this point in internet history, most consumers have seen websites making ridiculous claims for things like weight loss and even cognitive improvement. Consumers know anyone can say anything on their website, and they aren't quick to trust testimonials served up this way. Pulling in ratings from third-party websites your company doesn't control is a different matter. Reviews and ratings influence customers. This doesn't mean your business will sink if one unfair comment gets posted. It does mean, however, that consumers are interested in the overall sentiment they can learn from others who have had experiences with your brand.

Providing small reassurances is also helpful. Next to the button where someone is about to submit their email address to your website, consider saying something like, "Don't worry, we'll never sell your information," or, "You can easily unsubscribe if you don't absolutely love our monthly updates."

Saying the Right Thing

Enticement is an important element to consider as part of the conversion experience. For example, many people today feel that receiving a newsletter is not a good enough reason to give up their email addresses. "Sign up to receive our monthly newsletter" will more than likely not get a lot of response. Saying, "Receive monthly coupons you can use in our store," might. Or "Receive monthly instruction on making organically-sourced meals for your family," might work, too. Whenever you want someone to take an action on your website, consider dangling a carrot as part of the "ask."

Urgency can also be effective. Often customers are convinced to move forward, but they just don't feel like taking action now. They think, "Maybe if I wait, something better will come along." Keep in mind you are not only asking customers to make a positive decision in your direction, you are also asking them to make the decision about when to take action. That's why it works to create a case that helps consumers with this part of their decision. Give them a reason to do it now.

This can be tricky. Consumers have been put under this pressure so much by marketers, they can see right through a false urgency. Saying a sale ends Friday when customers know you would offer the same price next week can be risky. You could easily end up with a potential consumer walking away. Sometimes it helps to offer a positive add-on that rewards an immediate decision. For example, if you buy a sofa from us this week, you'll get a free lamp or half-price delivery. Airlines telling me there is only one seat left at a certain price helps move me along in making the purchase, as does a deadline in order to get early-bird pricing for a conference.

Adding just the right language to describe the final step may help increase your conversions as well. If you've done a good job showing your potential customer how you're going to solve their problem or make their life better, you've also painted a picture of what it will be like after they hire you. At the final moment, when you're asking them to take the next step, it can be useful to help them remember the promise of what lies ahead. You can reference the key psychological driver on the "Buy Now" button with language like "Start Saving Now," or "Begin Your Weight Loss Journey," or "Secure Your Future." Something as subtle as using the words, "Let's Go!" instead of "Submit" on the button that books your travel, for example, makes the experience even more enticing.

As I mentioned earlier, the right language can help provide clarity around the next step you're asking a customer to take. Everyone has had at least one bad experience talking to a pushy salesperson. For example, you call to get more information about a heat pump you're investigating, and the person answering the phone follows a script that makes you provide all your contact information before they'll give you any product information or pricing. What consumer doesn't dread being put in that situation? Assuring a customer this isn't going to happen makes it easier for them to act and call.

The Christmas Tree

Once a potential customer has a vision of what it will be like to become your client, you're in a great position. I clearly remember when my wife and I were shopping for our first home. Standing in what was soon to become our house, I asked my wife, "Now where would we put the Christmas tree?"

The realtor, who was standing nearby, had a big smile on her face. She said, "I just love when they ask the Christmas tree question! They always buy the house after they know where the tree goes!"

We laughed about it at the time, especially because my wife

and I had agreed in advance not to act too enthusiastic or appear too committed before we negotiated the price. But we clearly had a vision of living there, which is a powerful effect you would hope any potential customer experiences. Your marketing needs to create the "Christmas Tree Effect" at every opportunity.

This can be done in smaller ways. Certainty helps consumers make decisions and take action. For example, small businesses might consider adding photos of the staff member who answers the phone on the website's "Contact Us" page. A well-placed testimonial on such a page might increase the percentage of visitors who take action.

Death by Marketing - Part II

Let's return to the story of Randy and Mike.

Randy and Mike were now standing side by side, enjoying the view of the playground across the street, getting ready to wrap up their meeting. They were amused at how fast the kids were whizzing down the slide, many out of control by the time they got to the bottom.

Just behind that slide was another playground slide. A little girl had climbed the ladder and sat down, ready to slide. She went about three feet and stopped. The sap from a pine tree shading the slide had left a residue, which made this slide very unpopular on the playground.

"That's what my marketing strategy was like this year," Randy said. "I invested only at the beginning of my potential customers' experiences, and they heard about me, but I didn't set up other mechanisms to actually help them become my customers."

Making sure Randy truly understood, Mike pressed him a bit more. "So where do you go from here?"

Randy turned and picked up the four-page pile of notes he had taken from their prior meetings. "Well, first I'm going to cut my advertising budget by 75 percent. That will free up money to implement a different plan."

"Sounds good so far," Mike said, with encouragement.

"Next, I'm going to resurrect my email list and start a monthly campaign that tells stories of how I've helped create estate-quality outdoor landscapes on middle-class budgets," Randy said. "My customers are mostly middle to upper middle class, and they don't realize they really can afford to have amazing properties. People don't realize how much our work increases home values. My wife is a really good writer, and I know she'll jump at the chance to get involved in this project."

Mike seemed surprised that Randy came up with the idea so quickly. "I love it! Where can I sign up?" Mike asked. "Sounds great so far! What else are you planning?"

"I'm going to completely rebuild my website. But this time, I'm going to do it right," Randy said. "I'm going to use a digital marketing company that not only will build the right website, but will also partner with me over the next two years to refine it and make sure it is the lead generator I need, not just a pretty brochure."

Mike looked at Randy the way a proud father would look at his son.

Randy continued, "I'm also going to meet with my wife and one of our key employees who helps me with sales. I want to really drill down on the questions and concerns people have before they hire us. I'm also going to do some research online."

"Research?" Mike asked.

"Yes, I'm going to investigate how we're doing on search engines and make sure I'm easy to find, and I'm going to hire the right people to make sure we stay visible online. I want to make sure visitors have a good experience and become customers," Randy said.

"Like on a smartphone," Mike interrupted.

Randy blushed because he knew exactly what Mike meant. Randy's current website experience was extremely frustrating for mobile users.

"Yes!" Randy promised. "By the end of this year, my website is going to be a lead generation machine. Then I'm going to work on building the volume of traffic to it."

"Exactly," Mike said, smiling. "That's exactly what you need to do!"

CHAPTER SUMMARY

- Leaders must take care to understand the primary marketing problem they must solve.

- Viewing the consumer's purchasing decision journey as a series of dominos, leaders must recognize the importance of each phase and identify any areas of impasse.

- Leaders should recognize where there may be "friction" in the consumer's purchase decision journey.

- Businesses should consider the desired consumer mindset and the consumer thoughts and emotions that lead to a "yes."

QUESTION 5

What's the Thing That Sells the Thing?

I remember it like it was yesterday. My wife was sitting at the other end of the sofa, and she looked at me and smiled. At that moment, I knew she was the one for me. We were engaged a few weeks later. Many couples can recall magic moments similar to mine. It's a milestone experience from which there is no turning back—that point in the relationship that stands out above all the other dates, dinners, and conversations.

But this concept of a milestone experience also applies to business development and marketing. If a business leader can recognize a pattern in how customers might experience a "no turning back" moment, they may have a game-changing insight, one that will revolutionize the success of their marketing strategy.

Years back, I had a conversation about this with a client named Joan who was responsible for selling an expensive product. It was a complex sale that involved several decision-makers, took a long period of time, and required a lot of information. I asked her to identify which experiences or what part of the sales process she considered milestones. In other words, if she could just get her next prospect to do or to experience one thing, what would it be? What is that no-turning back experience?

In my clumsy attempt and frustration to guide her, I blurted out, "Joan, what's the thing that sells the thing?" Somehow, that language resonated with her and facilitated not only a productive marketing conversation, but also a new way of thinking for her and her teammates. As she began using this phrase within her organization and with my company's team, it became a silly phrase that represented what I have come to believe is one of the most powerful, yet underused, marketing concepts—identifying milestone experiences in your customers' journeys, then emphasizing and building marketing strategies around those experiences.

We've all had them. Remember when you took that puppy home for a trial period? Or how about when you asked to see the dessert menu because you were "curious."

Earlier in this book, we talked about Joe, who was trying to find a wife. It was obvious Joe needed to learn how to date rather than propose marriage as soon as possible. The business analogy was obvious. Now, we're shifting our focus to that one special date, when she knew Joe was the one for her. In business terms, what is that "no-turning-back experience," or in Joan's and my words, "the thing that sells the thing?"

Since that time, I've reflected on how many businesses have, perhaps unintentionally, used this powerful strategy. I know that I used it to solve a business problem 20 years ago—how to sell dressage horses to American buyers.

Selling Dressage Horses

I was once shortlisted with the United States Equestrian Team.

I   traveled nationally, giving riding clinics to dressage riders, and managed an active training center at home in Pennsylvania. In 1999, when health reasons prevented me from competing, I decided to step up my horse-selling activity to earn some money while I was starting another business. I became a contributing writer for a national dressage riding magazine, *Dressage Today*. I also built a website that ranked well on search engines, powered by the unique and helpful articles I was publishing for American buyers shopping for their next dressage horse.

The United States was filled with frustrated sport horse buyers who had wasted weekends and money on plane fares shopping domestically, one horse at a time. It was a time-consuming, expensive, and often futile approach to finding a good horse. The cost of airfare and hotel stays gobbled up buyers' budgets, and stories of failed horse-shopping trips were rampant in the industry.

My U.S.-based competitors were trying to sell dressage horses to these frustrated buyers and were struggling to stay in business. Their marketing process involved advertising, posting horses for sale online, sending horse videos to interested parties, then hoping someone would come to their farm to evaluate the horse.

The problem was this process rarely produced sales, especially for the time and money a seller had to put into it. To find success, I knew I'd need a better idea. What milestone experience could I create for buyers so they'd follow through and purchase a horse? I came up with the idea of taking buyers on a five-day dressage horse shopping trip to Europe. I knew from experience that if a qualified buyer boarded a plane and traveled around Holland and Germany with me, 95 percent of the time, they would buy a dressage horse. Trips to Europe produced sales. This became the guiding insight for all my marketing.

I wrote articles about picking good horses, shopping in Europe, and navigating a veterinary pre-purchase exam. I built a website with content that romanticized the idea of horse shopping in Europe. I explained that in Holland, a buyer could see 20 horses in a few days compared to seeing only one or two per week in the United States. I posted beautiful images of virtual inventory showcasing the types of horses shoppers would likely encounter and the typical price ranges. Customers could travel with me on a buying trip or simply opt to have me shop on their behalf, as Freddie Graves did for her 14-year-old daughter, Laura—who, like many 14-year-old riders, had dreams of someday riding in the Olympics.

Freddie reached out to me on her daughter's behalf, asking me to help find a special horse. At her request, I extended my upcoming buying trip one extra day to shop for a horse for young Laura. I found a promising young horse and Freddie and Laura approved. I couldn't have predicted the amazing outcome of that trip.

As I write this book, the most successful horse in the history of dressage riding in the United States is that horse, a handsome bay Dutch gelding named Verdades, ridden by this ambitious girl. Laura and Verdades broke all U.S. individual performance records in the 2018 Olympics, gained sponsorship from Deloitte, and attracted national media attention. This remarkable success story traces back to the conversation I had with Freddie after she found me online, read the articles I had written about horse shopping in Europe, and ultimately called me. She bought into the idea of shopping in Europe, the thing that sells the thing.

The rest is history.

Finding That Key Insight

I built that boutique business by answering the all-important question, "How can I develop a lead-generation system for selling dressage horses without going broke?" In my case, I had a key insight that if people traveled to Europe with me, a sale would almost always follow. Like many business leaders, I stumbled upon it through trial and error and looking for patterns of success.

Today, as I sit down with business leaders to talk about growing their businesses, I try to help them find their own key insight as I had found mine. I ask them, "What's 'the thing that sells the thing' for your industry?" What customer activity, experience, or emotional resolve creates that no-turning-back experience? Is it a visit to your showroom, the first free consultation, that amazing video on your website, or that free trial you're offering?

In the years working at my own digital marketing agency, I've discovered most business leaders and their sales teams hold key insights to their own best business development opportunities. Too often they don't realize the amazing opportunities they have in leveraging these insights for driving new business and, consequently, how these insights should direct their marketing strategy. Instead, they talk to marketing companies like mine about new ideas.

Business stakeholders usually know how new customers find their business. These patterns point to where sales come from and which marketing pathways they need to invest in and cultivate. Great marketing strategies are most often built around what already works and are powered by valuable insights into what creates sales for the business and "no-turning-back experiences" for customers.

A Tale of Two Non-Profits

Lancaster County, Pennsylvania, where I've lived my entire life, has more than its fair share of non-profits. As a local business owner, I am constantly solicited for donations. A few have won me over, but many more haven't. You may think those choices correlated to my belief system, but that's only partly true. It's about ownership. Like most donors, I believe some organizations are "mine" to support, while others are not. While many pull my heartstrings and align with my passions, they don't get my money. As I look back at how that came to be, how some helped me feel like an owner, I noticed a pattern.

One organization in my area comes to mind. They support disabled and handicapped citizens in the community, and I love what they do, but I've never sent them a dollar. Meanwhile, another non-profit in town called SWAN4Kids that serves children of incarcerated parents gets regular donations from me and my wife. How do they do it?

Whenever the disabled persons' non-profit contacts me, they ask for money. I think to myself, "I hope they get some donations. That's a nice cause, and (other) people should donate to it. I really hope they succeed in their fund-raising."

When SWAN4Kids first approached me, they asked for my advice. I felt honored, and I gave them some advice, which they used. From that point on, I felt like this organization's success was partly mine. Making donations to them became an easy decision for me. It was like a switch flipped in my brain. I felt like SWAN4Kids was my responsibility to care for, moving forward.

Of course, other nonprofits ask for donations, and they deserve them, too. But asking strangers for donations often proves to be frustrating, especially in a community like mine, which is crowded with solicitation messages. Forging a relationship by asking for my advice was the first "ask." Once that milestone was reached in my relationship with SWAN4Kids, this non-profit became my cause.

You Can Leave Your Kid Here

My sons attended a private Christian school near our home. During their years there, the school went from nearly going out of business to enjoying booming enrollment to having a waiting list in a short time. I'll discuss this further in other parts of this book, but one of the keys to their successful turnaround was perfecting their school tour.

All of the other private schools in the area gave tours, but we made it a milestone event. We did this by stopping by the classroom the child would potentially call their own, then allowing them to stay there and play with their soon-to-be classmates. It was all a well-choreographed experience engineered by our brilliant school tour guide, Kim. She would take the parents around our clearly inferior building, explaining that while we might not have all the bells and whistles found at other schools, we *did* have wonderful teachers, a great curriculum, and a nurturing environment. When Kim and the parents would arrive back at the classroom, the child would protest leaving. Their classmates were now begging them to stay. An emotional milestone was reached, and at that moment, sending the child to this school felt right to the parents.

Kim had a nearly 100 percent enrollment rate when parents took her tour. She understood providing parents with the experience of seeing their kids safe, happy, and well-adjusted was more powerful than the up-to-date chemistry lab the school's competitors had to offer.

Sellers of time-shares have this practice down to a science. For ridiculously low prices, potential buyers can enjoy beautiful accommodations by simply agreeing to sit through a sales presentation. Tanned, relaxed, and with their guard down, many unsuspecting couples have come home from those cheap vacations as time-share owners, a decision they never would have made otherwise. The week at the time-share is the pivotal event for buyers, and marketing for that industry focuses on "selling" a very inexpensive getaway (with a few strings attached).

Correlations

As you set out to discover your business's milestone experience, you may discover more than one. This certainly is true for students shopping for the right college. Spending time on a college campus is one of those student experiences that drives enrollment. A three-year study of 23,187 students conducted at Midwestern State University found students who visit campus are twice as likely to enroll as students who do not. Smart colleges market events and experiences that bring pre-college students to their locations. For colleges, the campus visit is one of those milestone experiences in a college student's selection process.

But the milestone event often isn't the last touch point a customer experiences before making a purchase decision. Let's say you're shopping for a new water dispenser for your office. With your budget and decision timeline, you're ready to buy today if you find a solution that seems like a good fit. You do a search on Google and then peruse the search results, looking at both the paid and organic listings. You see a few companies that seem worth investigating, and you click the one with numerous reviews. "That looks trustworthy," your subconscious assures you. You go to the website, which quickly informs you about the types of products they have and who uses them. So far, it seems like a good fit.

Next, you watch a video about how the product works, and you're excited because you're feeling like your search may be over. You click to buy the product and discover the price. It's about 20 percent more than you wanted to pay. Your gut makes you feel uncomfortable because you don't know what other options you have. But then your eye catches a link on the page that says, "Compare Other Options."

On this product comparison page, you see a list of typical types of office water solutions, their advantages, disadvantages, and typical price ranges. You quickly realize by looking at this chart that this is indeed the best fit, and saving money on another solution would leave you with regrets. A minute later, you've made the purchase. I'm quite confident if we looked at the user data for that website, we would see a correlation between one of your actions and the final purchase you made. In our example scenario, the video created the buying momentum that carried you through the rest of your purchasing steps. Companies often discover important correlations between certain actions taken on a website and buying decisions. It's important to recognize that a customer's milestone event might not be the last thing a person experiences before making a purchase. With careful analysis, this company realized that web visitors who watched the video had a 43 percent higher probability of making a purchase before leaving the website. Without that data, credit would have been given to the comparison chart, since that was the last action taken before the sale. The comparison chart was not the milestone event, it was simply there to reduce the consumer's "buying friction." In this case, the video sparked the excitement for the product and motivation to continue on the path toward a purchase.

The Danger of Asking for Big Steps

Every day, I receive emails from other companies who want to introduce themselves and their services to me. I don't know them, but they're asking for fifteen minutes of my time to discuss their offerings. I know the word "discuss" is code for "hard-sell," and there's no way on Earth I'd ever agree to give my time to a stranger who emails me.

Business-to-business marketing and other high-value decisions tend to be more complex. The more complex a sale is, the more steps it needs. Some businesses know if they can convince a decision-maker to talk to them, they might make a sale. A day doesn't go by without a well-meaning salesperson emailing or calling my office requesting a 15-minute phone meeting with me to introduce their product or services. Giving up time in my work day is a big "ask," and I never agree to it when asked by a stranger. In a complex sale, a human connection or other sources of deeper trust need to be made earlier in the sales journey before a big ask is attempted.

The buyer's journey should never make the consumer take big steps. In fact, the more small steps you can construct that lead up to that milestone experience, the better the chance you'll create a business development system that works.

As you're designing your website or any part of your marketing campaign, making the right impression and providing information aren't the only factors to consider. You have to go beyond content architecture. You need to employ user-experience (UX) architecture, and you must have empathy to be a good UX architect. You must understand the audience, their needs, and how they want to discover a product or service, and you need to choreograph those steps.

The key, however, is to make sure each step is a realistic "ask" and a reasonable next step. It must be achievable to appeal to even the most fickle consumers.

Marketing is Not "The Plan"

Recently, I attended a board meeting for a small private college.

During the meeting, we voted on and passed an initiative to expand and grow some educational offerings. I was surprised at the lack of concern among the other attendees, peers I considered very experienced business people involved with large and successful companies. No one asked, "How are we going to take this to market?" They saw what seemed to be a hefty marketing budget in the business plan, and apparently that was enough to convince everyone to vote "yes" on the motion to proceed without deeper scrutiny.

I've worked with enough business initiatives to understand that a good business idea is not enough to ensure success. In this case, we had done our due diligence and had hired a consulting firm to validate a market demand for our proposed offerings. But what was the plan to take it to market?

There is a common misconception that marketing is a stand-alone solution for taking a product or service to market. Companies frequently bring a budget to the marketing company and expect a miracle in return. The truth is, great success stories not only have the right product, but also a brilliant plan to take it to the marketplace.

Marketing must be in service of a business development plan to be successful. Without the plan, marketing is only providing exposure. In today's crowded advertising world, marketing alone is likely to run any business right into the red.

That's why I stopped working for start-ups years ago. I can remember one instance in particular. A group of ambitious and smart entrepreneurs met in my conference room asking me to take their cool, new, externally-hosted VoIP (voice-over IP) business phone solution to market for them (on a very modest budget). They made it clear they were going to hold me accountable to get results.

When I asked them which market sector was going to be receptive, why people would agree to change systems, and what made their offering special, they gave me blank stares. When I asked them about the anatomy of the sales experience for their clients, they didn't know. When I asked them what concerns needed to be addressed before a potential client would move forward, they didn't have any insights to offer. They believed we could somehow just do some "marketing," and their business would grow. I tried to explain to them that it doesn't work like that, especially for an unknown start-up selling a product many people didn't understand. In the end, we referred them to another company and wished them well.

Any good business plan needs a valid solution to a market need *and* a way to take it to market. This is a common mistake I see leaders make who have minimal business development experience. They believe marketing is a substitute for a business development plan. It's not.

For example, if I'm in the business of selling dressage horses and hire a marketing company to help me, they would most likely develop a good brand image for my company and then help me buy media to create awareness for the horses I have for sale. Buyers would call me and ask what I had for sale. I'd tell them, and after a long conversation, I'd send them a video. Based on my experience, most of those leads would go nowhere after that. The remaining few prospective customers might visit my farm to try horses but probably wouldn't buy a horse.

However, if I took the time to develop the plan around the insight that a trip to Europe is "the thing that sells the thing," that would radically change my marketing approach. I would design all my efforts around that business development plan. For example, I would write articles like, "How To Shop for Horses in Europe," rather than general articles about dressage horses. I would design a website about the horse-buying trip experience, rather than about current horses I had for sale.

Go to Market Plans Before Marketing Plans

I recently sat down with Sheila, a talented business consultant. She had a great idea for an online training program and wanted my advice on where and how to advertise it. A few minutes into the conversation, I asked her, "How do you imagine you'll get new clients? Do you picture people searching for this, finding you, then signing up?"

The answer to my question was self-evident. "No." Sheila was offering a new type of training tool to promote better relationships in the workforce. Something that didn't exist on the market. Because of that, people weren't searching for it, so search strategies were off the table. I gently suggested we talk about how she planned to take this to market before spending money on advertising for something people didn't understand.

"What's your plan on how to win new business? As your advertising generates new contacts, do you have a plan for converting them, or for staying in touch with them, like trickle email marketing campaigns?" I asked.

She didn't.

Leaders typically begin focusing on the top of the marketing funnel, advertising, when they want to build a lead-generation system. But savvy leaders start with a more ground-tactical plan. They look at past success stories and discern a series of likely experiences that captures the interest of a targeted audience and takes them to a no-turning-back experience.

In Sheila's case, she was an in-demand speaker for business groups. If she were to use that exposure to leverage the relationships she built at her speaking engagements using any number of marketing best practices, she'd certainly develop her business far more effectively than by advertising to a broad group of strangers.

Go-to-market plans need to precede marketing strategies. Many times, leaders believe marketing strategies are a substitute for go-to-market plans, but they're not. Often, this practical planning for business development dictates radically different marketing strategies and makes them far more effective.

My friend David is a great example. He is an expert at business succession planning, and he discovered he gets most of his new business from referrals from attorneys, financial planners, and bankers. With this insight, he developed a business networking monthly event called "Breakfast with David" specifically for business people in these three industries. This invitation-only event became a who's-who network for some key business people in the community. As the founder and gatekeeper, David was at the center of every conversation and activity. Specific conversations he had with attendees became his no-turning-back experience. Building these relationships provided the platform over time to have those conversations. This approach became a highly successful, ongoing source of leads for David's business.

David's marketing was all devoted to building this network. Had he asked a marketing company to provide leads, they might have bypassed this excellent and successful plan. They might have spent too many of David's marketing dollars trying to get strangers to express interest in David's services. Instead, David was able to direct all of his marketing dollars toward promoting in-person networking events.

What's the Thing That Sells the Thing?

As you consider how you're going to invest time and money in your marketing and business development, be sure to take time to reflect on an activity, an event, a conversation, or any experience that has a high correlation to someone becoming your customer. In my experience, this can take some time and thought. It's often a good idea to bring in leadership teams as well as salespeople for help. Make sure whoever answers the phones for incoming sales leads is around the table when you have this conversation.

Don't worry if you have more than one strategy. For example, we have a client who is a furniture manufacturer. He recognized those potential clients (furniture retailers) who toured his manufacturing facility frequently signed up to be resellers. He also noticed more distant prospects often signed up after they spoke with a salesperson and ordered wood samples. These actions became important milestones in the client-conversion pathway.

It's important to answer the question, "What's it going to take to get the prospective customer to that all-important milestone event from which there is no turning back?" This isn't easy to answer. As you figure it out through trial and error, you are nearly guaranteed to find and build a reliable and powerful lead-generation system, even for selling dressage horses!

CHAPTER SUMMARY

- There are milestone events in a consumer's decision journey that are "no-turning-back" experiences, after which consumers nearly always become customers.

- While marketers typically focus on activities that lead to a sale, working toward those milestones instead may be a more successful strategy.

- Identifying a marketing milestone may help direct a very different marketing approach, even a different business model.

- Milestone moments can often be identified when leaders consider which activities and experiences have led to "no-turning-back" mindsets for their existing customers.

- Milestone moments can take many forms, like well-orchestrated in-person events, well-designed conversations between salespeople and clients, and even compelling website content.

- Businesses should establish business development plans before marketing plans. They are not the same thing.

- The best milestone events don't require the potential customer to take too big of a step or make too frightening of a decision.

How Will People Hear About Us?

Business leaders frequently come to a point in their business growth where they ask, "Where should we advertise?" I suggest a better question: "How will people hear about us?" I've had two recent experiences with small business owners who had to address this problem.

Jane was an ambitious young entrepreneur with a new product that seemed like the next big thing. She had invented, developed, and taken to market a shampoo that contained a proprietary blend of antioxidants. With daily use, customers reported their hair not only took on a new level of sheen, they also claimed the product was boosting their immune systems. Everyone Jane talked to agreed she was really onto something. Yet two years into the project, Jane was at an impasse.

She was out of cash because sales hadn't taken off in the first year. While she was eager to take her product to market, she didn't know where to advertise. All the options she explored were too expensive. She only made $5 profit on a sale, and while spending thousands of dollars, she just wasn't able to see enough sales relative to the cash she was burning through for advertising. Jane needed another solution for getting the word out about her product.

Anthony had all the signs of being a successful financial planner. He had a unique service model that used technology to keep his clients more informed than his competitors. His existing customers were really happy with him. However, he hadn't figured out how to get new clients. He tried advertising in the newspaper, but the responses were mostly calls from people who wanted to sell radio, billboard space, and TV advertising. Potential customers weren't responding.

No matter what he tried, he couldn't get leads through advertising. He even tried advertising online through Google. Nothing seemed to work for lead generation. His business revenues were flat for the last three years, and he hadn't come close to reaching his company's growth goals.

Why wasn't his business growing? What do both of these business owners have in common?

They don't know how to create awareness affordably and effectively. They might have an excellent business product or service waiting for new customers, but their business models don't have a plan for affordably or effectively generating new business.

This is important. Businesses succeed or fail based in part on how well leaders solve this problem. As we discussed in the previous chapter, inexperienced leaders naively believe that budgeting for advertising is a substitute for a go-to-market plan, but most of the time it isn't. That's where Jane and Anthony went wrong. Jane assumed there would be an affordable traditional advertising opportunity, but there wasn't. Her go-to-market strategy might have been effective product placement with retailers, or using influencer marketing. Anthony assumed advertising would bring him leads, but it didn't. His type of business awareness strategy will probably always be one that involves person-to-person interactions, not paid advertising.

Smart business leaders don't assume they can "advertise" a product or service into success. Even more, they don't assume simply advertising is the entire plan. Instead, they explore other ideas for creating awareness, plans that best leverage their business's time and money, plans that may or may not include advertising.

The question, "Where should we advertise?" often makes unsound assumptions. Jane's and Anthony's stories illustrate that. In this chapter, we'll cover new and outside-the-box ideas and questions that might inspire you to lead highly successful awareness campaigns for your business.

How Many Leads Do I Need?

Several years ago, I was sitting in the office of one of the most talented college recruiters I've ever met. Jordan and his team had a clear goal to reach—to enroll 350 students in the next eight months. He had a great track record for exceeding his goals.

As Jordan pulled his team into the room, I leaned forward and observed with great interest, so I could unpack the secret of his success. Within a minute, I had my answer. Jordan made no attempts at hiding his strategy, and I'll never forget how he explained it.

"We only need 350 students," he started. "You know how we're going to do it?" he asked. "One student at a time!"

Jordan understood that recruiting 350 students wasn't the same as getting two million new software users, or five million new mobile phone subscribers. He didn't need to market in the same way that mass marketers do. Instead, he needed to make strong efforts to about 2,000 leads which, given the school's history, wouldn't be hard to find.

Most small businesses somehow miss this very basic insight that Jordan had instinctively. They believe the best strategies are the ones large brands use. They feel they should campaign for the largest advertising budget possible, then spend every dime to create broad awareness to build the brand and get leads. When the plan doesn't work, they blame their budget. "If we had more money for marketing, we could meet our enrollment numbers," they rationalize.

There is an incredibly important lesson we all need to take away from Jordan's example. Before we set out to spend money on advertising, we need to ask ourselves, "How much exposure do we really need?" That very important question is seldom asked.

Jordan knew he didn't need to run advertisements in national magazines as some of his competitors were doing. He knew students within a hundred-mile radius were most likely to enroll. He needed to engage in marketing and activities to enroll those candidates.

Guided by these insights, Jordan used his marketing budgets for networking opportunities and traveling budgets for trips to high schools and other key opportunities to meet students one at a time until they had 350 recruits.

When a business leader needs to ramp up the number of leads coming in the door, it's tempting to overspend in creating awareness. But for many small- and medium-sized businesses and many business-to-business industries, advertising dollars are easily wasted trying to reach far more people than necessary. Smart leaders first determine how many leads they actually need to meet their sales objectives. That first question will be a helpful guide in answering other important questions.

Who Wants This and Why?

One of the biggest problems with traditional advertising is that businesses are often paying to reach broader audiences than needed. Without narrowing the target, businesses pay for far more people to see their ads than they need to. For example, if a local business has a billboard for a lawn mower shop, thousands and thousands of people who aren't going to buy a lawn mower are driving by and seeing it. And in most cases, advertising prices are based on the traffic count.

That's why targeting is always the primary factor to consider when you're paying for exposure for your brand, product, or service. Smart businesses pay for exposure to the most targeted audiences in order to leverage their marketing dollars. But targets can be tricky to fully understand, let alone reach.

When Jack came to me for help with his high-end men's clothing store, one of the first things we discussed was his ideal customer. I naturally assumed it was a male businessman between 30 and 55 who lived within a 20-mile distance to his store. I was wrong. Actually, to a great degree, he targeted women. Most men brought their wives, girlfriends, and even an occasional mother or administrative assistant with them to the store. Jack learned his marketing was more effective when he also targeted certain groups of women who influenced the decisions of men in their lives.

The same is true for every retirement community or elder care business I've spoken with. They consistently tell me an important audience to reach are the baby boomers who are helping their parents make a decision on where to move.

Most business owners I speak with are fairly confident about their target audience and who this is. But several years ago, after hearing a game-changing presentation from my friend Susan Baier, founder of Audience Audit, I began to think differently about target audiences.

Susan recounted a story about a manufacturer of home

fragrance products. After conducting attitudinal segmentation research, the brand gained some extremely valuable insights about their target audience. While they had believed their audience was largely upper-income, middle-aged women who bought their products because of their complex and unique fragrances, they learned their audience was much more diverse—especially when it came to the reasons they were buying home fragrance items.

The research identified important and statistically sound segments, each buying to fulfill very different needs. As they'd expected, some buyers focused on fragrance above all else because it helped them reinforce or reset their mood at home. Some buyers were looking for a gift to impress, which had to come from a recognized premium brand and have expensive-looking packaging. Still others were looking for a product to help them create the look they wanted in their home, and color and style were more important than fragrance. The candle company learned they could craft specific messages for specific attitudinal segments of their formerly broad audience of buyers. With that insight, smarter targeting, messaging, and spending became possible. When business leaders understand why someone is motivated to buy a product or use a service, they're often paving the way toward identifying powerful and impactful marketing. For example, this company might work harder to intercept an audience of "gift-buyers" by advertising in gift magazines and appearing on gift suggestion lists online.

Getting clarity about the various attitudes and consumers' emotional drivers often provides needed insights into where and how a business should create awareness. Even more, this clarity about target audiences will provide important guidance regarding the language a business should use in their advertising.

How Can We Leverage Good Will?

I recently met with several partners in a financial advisory firm. They freely admitted they'd done a terrible job in marketing themselves over the years, but then pointed out they had grown in spite of it. That's not uncommon. A great business, one that delivers an excellent product or service that evokes more word-of-mouth, typically finds its own organic growth because of what people say.

The opposite is also true. Businesses that don't deliver a great product or service and earn a bad reputation, can't make up for it with marketing. When a business is established and doing well, the first strategy to explore involves answering this question: "How can we leverage the good will of our existing customers?" While some highly regulated industries like financial advisories are restricted on how they acquire, use, or even allow customer testimonials, that's almost always a great place to start.

Word of mouth

Every business dreams of new leads streaming in from organic, word-of-mouth driven customer referrals. And many small businesses rely heavily on this type of lead origination. But few businesses actually work at building word-of-mouth strategies.

In their ground-breaking book, *Talk Triggers, The Complete Guide to Creating Customers With Word of Mouth,* Jay Baer and Daniel Lemin unpack how businesses can be intentional with operational details that are catalysts for epic word of mouth results. Whether featuring a ridiculously large menu like the Cheesecake Factory restaurant, or dumping delightfully more french fries in your brown bag at Five Guys Burgers, some brands have brilliantly instigated their audiences to talk about them. These and countless other inspiring examples in Baer's and Lemin's book demonstrate the powerful opportunity for brands to approach awareness challenges using this strategy. Brands that fail to do this, as these authors point out, will be "taxed" with the cost of advertising.

Online reviews

The past decade has seen a significant increase in consumer involvement with online reviews. More and more, people are posting about their experiences with brands and reading what others have written before they make purchase decisions.

Most businesses have many happy customers in their wake but haven't made any effort to garner positive feedback or to leverage the positive sentiments of their raving fans. For years, as I've brought this up to clients, I've gotten emotional reactions. It's common to hear a tirade about an unfair review that an unreasonable customer or even a dishonest competitor wrote about them, and their inability to have it taken down. I try to explain that while reviews are sometimes unfair, they are also influential and can't be ignored. Both good and bad reviews and online posts are going to happen whether or not businesses make review-building part of their awareness strategy. No matter how upsetting reviews can be to a business leader, the answer is never to bury one's head in the sand. Wise leaders take a proactive approach to making sure their many happy customers overshadow the few inevitable unhappy customers.

If a business has a fairly high volume of customers each month, and they're able to collect emails or mobile phone numbers from their customers, they should consider implementing customer feedback software to help. There are a variety of programs available to businesses that can be a big help in requesting and tracking customer feedback and online review activity. But software solutions aren't for everyone.

Businesses with a low volume of monthly customers, for example, a roofer or solar energy installation company, might be better off conducting their own surveys. Then they can follow up individually with customers, asking happy customers to write online reviews and addressing concerns for the occasional unhappy customer.

As disappointing as it is to get a bad review now and then, keep in mind a perfect score is not actually the best score. Consumer studies consistently show that somewhere between 4 and 5 stars tends to be the most positively influential. Perhaps when readers see some of the negative reviews, they feel they've done sufficient research and are ready to make the decision to move forward.

Businesses should monitor and respond to reviews to show potential customers they genuinely care about their customers' experiences. Certainly, some comments don't warrant a response— for example, spam and hateful speech or inappropriate content. Comments like these should be flagged and reported to the review site. However, when a customer presents a heartfelt comment online, a wise and timely response from the business is advised.

Testimonials

Getting reviews is more complicated for some businesses and industries. Marketers in the medical industry, for example, are not permitted to respond to complaints because of privacy laws. But even highly regulated industries may have some options. While not as powerful as reviews on third-party websites, carefully selected testimonials in the form of short quotes placed on a website can be influential. For example, a testimonial about Dr. Smith might appear on her website's bio page. When a visitor is considering making contact with Dr. Smith's office, that testimonial might be the extra bit of encouragement needed for a potential client to pick up the phone. But keep in mind even the shadiest websites post testimonials, and even naive consumers doubt they're true. That's why it's important to only post testimonials that are relevant and interesting. This makes them more influential, though they'll be trusted less than testimonials and reviews posted on third-party websites like Yelp and Google.

Many successful businesses are finding success in creating video testimonials and using them on their websites, in emails, and alongside other communications. These don't have to be overly staged, but they should have good sound quality. The less they sound staged and commercial-like, the better.

Businesses are sometimes reluctant to ask their customers to help them out in this way. In our experience, happy customers are frequently enthusiastic advocates for a business, and many times, they're very willing to say something positive in front of a camera for a testimonial video. Keep in mind that, like getting reviews, the best time to ask for a testimonial is when the customer has a fresh smile on their face.

Referral programs

Besides reviews and testimonials, there's a third successful method many leaders have implemented to leverage the good reputation of their companies: a well-designed referral program.

As I write this, I'm enduring ongoing discomfort from the invisible braces I ordered online. I have a friend to blame for this. She referred me with a discount code worth several hundred dollars to encourage me to get started. Did she pay for my discount? No, the braces company paid me, and they also paid her. This clever company gave her the exact encouragement she needed to make a referral at the right time. I know this because they did it to me, too. Just as I got my new kit, and I was ready to begin my journey to perfect teeth, they sent me an email suggesting I "share a smile with a friend." They offered to give a very generous discount to anyone I chose. On top of that, they offered me a $100 discount on the amount I still owed if my referral was successful.

How perfect was this? I got to be a hero and give someone the best coupon they've ever received, *and* I got to enjoy a $100 discount. That was incentive enough for me to bite on their offer, even if it meant suggesting to a friend that his teeth were less than perfect. But I did it because I loved the product and because this company facilitated a seamless referral experience for me to use.

Keep in mind customers will rarely be manipulated or bribed to make a referral if they don't genuinely love their experience and feel positive about making a recommendation. I loved the product, and I thought the whole online braces concept was as great as the excellent user experience the company created from beginning to end. I wouldn't have participated in the referral program if I didn't think the company was awesome.

That's why review initiatives, testimonials, and referral programs only work if your business is worthy of them. In other words, these strategies only get traction if customers are really impressed with the products or services your business offers. A smart leader always works hardest at developing loyal, raving fans. Once that is done, the possibility of leveraging that good will becomes greater.

Business leaders should make sure their companies are leveraging their happy customers in every way they can. The power of a good word from a trusted source will have a far more positive impact than any clever marketing slogan. That's why this marketing concern is so important to consider. Best of all, it's an opportunity that will cost little more than some time and planning.

Who Else Knows Our Audience?

Getting customer referrals can be a powerful boost, but in some industries, peer-to-peer referrals are difficult to obtain. I remember when one of our financial advisors told us his high-net-worth clients were reluctant to make referrals, even though they were very satisfied with his work. His clients felt they would be betraying a friend if they referred them for help with their finances.

In my company, we've also run into resistance when asking for clients to make referrals. We found many of our clients felt we were their best-kept secret and wanted to keep it that way. Some reported feeling that our growth might result in their getting less of our time and attention. It made them reluctant to make referrals.

While it wasn't easy to do, we built a referring partner network, and it proved to be one of our greatest marketing discoveries. We forged authentic relationships with business people who had connections and influence with businesses we hoped would hire us. We befriended owners of programming shops, branding companies, business coaches, and manufacturers whose retailers needed marketing help. We offered referral incentives to those who wanted them and doled out generous thanks and notes of appreciation to all. We held regular networking lunches at our office when we invited our family of referring partners and provided interesting educational presentations about what was new in the internet marketing world. We communicated regularly to stay front-of-mind with them.

When businesses ask me for help reaching potential customers, I suggest they first consider who else has a relationship of trust with those specific audiences. Who else knows people they want to reach?

Then I ask them to consider why a potential referring partner would want to make a recommendation. For example, we partnered with branding agencies. At the time, we didn't engage in branding services specifically. Meanwhile, branding agencies had clients who frequently asked for help with SEO, which meant they needed a reliable referral option to recommend. Sharing leads with one another was a positive move for everyone and provided encouraging growth for our company.

We assumed, as many do, that everyone would want money as an incentive for making referrals, but we were wrong. Some seemed embarrassed to discuss financial incentives because they were hoping for a different payoff. They were investing in a relationship, returned affection, loyalty, or favors. We learned to bring this up in a sensitive manner, as offering to pay referring partners may feel like it is cheapening your business relationship with them, especially if they are partnering with you for noble or sentimental reasons.

My experience with referrals has taught me that while some individuals are highly motivated by financial incentives, in many cases, payment is the grease on the wheels for referrals but not the engine that drives them. People who hold a business in high regard will make referrals to it, and smart leaders are intentional about making that happen.

Where Should We Meet Them?

Often businesses can build successful awareness strategies by crafting effective "ground-tactical" business development networking events. When executed well, networking events are an effective tactic for creating awareness and meaningful engagement with potential customers. Essentially, a business network creates awareness for them.

A private Christian school in my area executed this tactic very effectively. Their key insight was that stay-at-home mothers of pre-school age children were sometimes desperate for out-of-home activities that were kid-safe and mom-friendly. This school offered a weekly event called "Tails and Tunes."

They brought miniature horses on the school property and had them waiting under large shade trees next to the parking lot. Moms and their kids and current kindergarten students and teachers gathered to pet these patient little ponies while a teacher read stories. Afterward, everyone went into the school to enjoy light refreshments.

Do you think a high percentage of these parents enrolled their children at this school the following year? Yes, they did, and it's easy to see why. Their children were already familiar with the school, the kindergarten teacher, and the classroom. They even met current kindergarten students. While other competing schools were spending thousands of dollars on billboards and newspaper advertisements, this school spent nearly nothing and out-performed every Christian school in the county in its year-over-year enrollment. Mothers told mothers about this program, and the awareness campaign was incredibly effective.

My company engaged in a similar strategy. We genuinely love helping businesses, so offering free educational lunches and speaking to local business groups was a natural fit for us. This opportunity to build relationships with key members of the business community rapidly led to tremendous business growth.

Not every business has local clientele. National companies able to create cult-like followings achieve the same thing, where people are attracted and united around a common interest, passion, or point of view. Red Bull has done a brilliant job at this. The adrenaline-filled Red Bull fans watch, relate to, and even help create amazing videos of breathtaking stunts done by...you guessed it...people who drink Red Bull. The best type of positive awareness is free, and smart businesses look for ways to engage their existing contacts and networks.

Other national and international companies have successfully created networking events in conjunction with conventions or conferences. My company has sponsored invitation-only breakfasts at industry conventions where we've made 30-minute educational presentations to a hand-picked audience of prospects. Other brands have sponsored after-hours parties, private product unveilings, even golf outings in conjunction with conferences.

Strategic Interception

Many business owners view their marketing budgets as expenses. But savvy businesses turn that perspective around and position marketing opportunities as profit centers or investments. That happens when businesses learn how to execute highly targeted advertising. Traditionally, targeting has been thought of in categories, such as location, gender, and socioeconomic factors. But if we think about marketing in terms of *creating experiences* rather than just making impressions, another targeting aspect becomes possible: *timing*.

Kraig Kramers understood the power of timing. Kraig was a former CEO of Snapper, the lawnmower manufacturer. In a speech given several years back and shortly before his death, he shared his amazing story at a business seminar I was fortunate to attend. In 1991, the year prior to Kraig becoming CEO, the floundering company reported $54 million in pre-tax losses. A year later, they turned a profit of $13 million.

Kraig's entire marketing strategy was built around one key insight: people shop for lawn mowers when it is raining. Snapper coordinated efforts using data from the National Weather Service and ran radio ads where and when it was raining in the United States. According to Kramers, they were able to get a return on their marketing dollars 10 times greater than their competition.

Kraig used the most powerful type of targeting available to businesses that want to capture the interest of a motivated audience. He used timing, and so can you, even without an insight about weather and shopping. How? By having a strong presence on Google.

Any business can use timing as a key advertising strategy by being front-of-mind at just the right time. Today, that's online. When potential customers are making purchase decisions they look for answers and options on search engines. At the time of writing this book, Google was the most-used search engine in the world, and that's especially true for mobile search.

Google is a business's most critical platform to consider. Since so many consumers have smartphones with them throughout the day, spontaneous research has become a normal behavior. By understanding that someone in the general population may suddenly become a "targeted prospect" through personal circumstance, businesses can make sure they are positioned to be found *when and where* people are searching online.

If my home's water heater is spewing water into my basement, I am suddenly the target audience for several local plumbers. But which one will get my call? The one who has organized themselves to be in front of me when I'm seeking a solution.

I pick up my smartphone and search for "water heater replacement." One company in particular appears in several spots on the search results page. I had a problem to solve at a particular time and was ready to give any business with the right solution my full attention. I chose the company that seemed to be the authority. They had an ad at the top of the page, their business was listed right below the map on the local search engine results page, and they had many positive reviews. That's targeting at its finest, and in essence, it's great timing!

Sadly, many other companies I passed over that day spent a good bit of money trying to get in front of me. But I ignored their messages because I didn't have a need when they interrupted me with their offers. On my drive home from work, that radio advertisement and the billboard display from other water heater companies didn't have much effect on my ultimate choice as a consumer. I didn't have a problem to solve during those moments. The company with a strong presence on Google won my business. They had the right timing.

My personal demographics didn't matter (race, age, income). What mattered was that I had a problem and was looking for the best way to solve it. When I have a problem, I want a solution *now*. The business that best understands that and prepares to be part of my solution wins. Today, that battle is won and lost on search engines.

By now, most business owners understand paid search advertising versus organic search. For paid search, businesses use Google's ad platform to bid on specific keywords customers might potentially use in their search queries. You don't pay to appear in Google's organic search results. Instead, you employ search engine optimization (SEO)—a collection of tactics that raises the chances your web pages will rank higher.

Most businesses don't realize the distinction between local SEO and national SEO. While similarities exist between the two, local search engine optimization has many technical aspects and is a specialized area of expertise. In my experience, many local business leaders have unrealistic expectations for SEO. For example, a local furniture store owner might want to rank nationally when Google users search for the word "chair." Instead, a realistic goal might be to make sure anyone searching for furniture in the immediate area can easily learn about the store, get directions, see some nice pictures, read reviews, and click to call.

When an experienced business leader engages an internet marketing firm, they're careful to determine whether it's good at national or local SEO. Don't be too quick to believe any agency is good at both, unless they have a large team and specialists devoted to each discipline. Smart leaders find a good match for their business type.

May I Interrupt You, Please?

In my experience, business leaders are constantly on the lookout for places to advertise. I'm convinced part of the attraction is vanity. As a business owner, it feels satisfying to see that billboard or full-page spread in print. But it's important not to let satisfaction blind you to the fact that it may not be bringing the return on investment you should be demanding.

Well-timed advertising interruptions can also happen mid-sale. For example, years back when I was buying a toy for my son for Christmas, the e-commerce website asked me if I wanted batteries. I hadn't thought of it, but I did need batteries. I'd never want to be the bad dad who forgot the batteries on Christmas morning. Good businesses understand how additional services or products coincide with a purchase decision that's already happening. Asking for the right thing at the right time is a proven way to create exposure for your product or service.

Many companies have used Facebook to introduce me to new gadgets and products. I'm relaxed, catching up on what's going on with my Facebook friends, when I discover an intriguing key organizer, travel pillow, or miracle vitamin that demands my attention. Minutes later, I've watched the compelling video, gotten enough information on an informative website, and ordered the gadget I discovered only a few minutes ago.

Reaching me on Facebook with an entertaining concept, especially when coupled with an intriguing video, frequently lures me into an impulse purchase because I'm relaxed, a bit vulnerable, and want to be entertained. In this case, the sellers understand my frame of mind and tailor their offering accordingly. As business leaders ask their teams to think about the timing of their advertising, everyone is guided into making better decisions about not only when, but where they might most effectively create exposure.

Creating Awareness by Being Helpful

Answering questions audiences are asking is an approach that always passes the test. It has proven to be a consistent winner in the digital age, and I don't expect it will ever go out of style.

One of our clients, Diane, did a great job at this. She initially came to us with a big problem. Her former SEO company had used some aggressive tricks to get her website to rank. A Google algorithm update penalized her site severely for these tricks. As a result, her website's pages were nowhere to be found in Google's search results. Her kitchen cabinet business was going to close in the near future if she didn't turn things around. Aside from undoing her former SEO company's damage, my team helped Diane launch a marketing campaign that made her business so successful, she couldn't keep up with sales. Here's why it worked.

Diane began by asking the people who handle incoming leads what questions customers were asking that week. Then we helped her make a video that addressed those questions. Within a year, her videos were found by more and more people who had questions about kitchen cabinet installation. Within two years, she had tens of thousands of YouTube subscribers, which generated more leads than her sales team could handle.

Diane didn't lead with a fancy tagline. She didn't create a unique advertising theme. She simply began helping a potential audience. More importantly, she worked hard at understanding specifically how she could be more helpful.

This same principle applies to any business that produces content as part of their business development plan. It's unwise to believe content marketing should focus on how often you publish content. Smart leaders know to produce content that brings value to their target audience.

And there's an opportunity to take this even further. On top of identifying and answering customers' questions, a business can deliver valuable insights. Insights are more than answers. They provide a deeper look at solutions and often uncover problems or opportunities customers didn't realize they had or were soon to experience.

As a business is considering how they might interrupt people, they might be well-guided by asking themselves another important question: "How can we exceed our audience's expectations with insights?"

Spammers and Car Dealers

I frequently receive emails from strangers around the world. They say things like, "We can get you to top of Google" (bad grammar intentional). I have a full-time front desk employee in charge of blocking calls from telemarketers. Some lie and say they are returning my call, they are a family member or a friend, or that I'm expecting their call.

Perhaps I'm a bit extreme, but I will never hire or even entertain a sales call from a company that creates exposure this way. Why? That's the way unscrupulous and desperate companies reach clients. Sure, there are some good companies that paid someone to get leads for them this way, but I have no way of knowing who they are. I associate spammers and telemarketers with the types of vendors I don't want to partner with. I categorically dismiss all of these potential vendors because of the way they chose for me to hear about them.

Make no mistake about it. Audiences make associations.

As I'm writing this, I'm shopping for a used car. I associate good outcomes with certain local dealerships and bad outcomes with some of our shady local vendors. Of course, I know there are good cars on the lots of shady dealers, and some bad cars in the hands of honest car sellers. But I, like most consumers, make "wholesale associations." Even if they aren't completely logical or accurate, they drive my buying decisions.

That's why smart businesses stop and think about how any type of advertising might create an unfortunate association. Before agreeing to a cold-calling telemarketing contract or using irritating pop-ups on a website that ruin users' smartphone browsing experiences, stop to think about how a customer really wants to be treated. Before advertising a discount, think about how that might be perceived, even on a subconscious level. Before booking a venue for a networking event, consider other brands that might also use the venue. Association is a powerful and often underestimated factor in influencing your audience.

I Can't Get That Song Out of My Head!

While most business leaders are asking their marketing teams where they should be advertising, smart leaders ask how they can make advertising sticky. In the past, we couldn't help but sing along to those catchy ad jingles. I remember the days when my friends would complain, "I can't get that song out of my head!" after hearing an advertisement jingle too many times. I believe most marketers agree that today, audiences find them more irritating than influential. However, creating lingering awareness is still a powerful approach.

When a leader insists their stakeholders develop a plan to make advertising "sticky," the results will likely be better. Digital technology is a great place to start because it makes it possible to track user behavior and follow up with potential customers. For example, if a user visits a certain page on a business's website, that business can make sure an advertisement appears on other websites the user visits in the weeks that follow. This is called retargeting, and businesses that advertise online should consider integrating some form of this.

Besides follow-up using technology, businesses can create stickiness using the right messaging. They can advertise with thought-provoking ideas that stick. For example, my company tells clients we do Near-User Marketing.® That's not a term people have heard before, and the cognitive dissonance created from hearing this makes people pause and remember that my company specializes in helping businesses reach local audiences.

Regardless of what type of approach you use to make your advertising sticky, it's important to keep people focused on a single idea. If a business has several value propositions, they may need to pick one in order to have success. Businesses that inject one line of thought about their products or services and change it the following week will only cause confusion. For example, if a builder promotes "a new home in six months, guaranteed," and next month says, "the right builder for the right price," they'll confuse the audience, even if both are true. One minute the customer thought they understood this company as the one that would "get it done," now they're being told the company is the "affordable" one.

Customers only have one mental file for you, and they won't create two files for your products and services. It's important to understand who you are up front, how you're going to communicate it, and to stick with the plan.

Automate Like a Human

More and more businesses are understanding how important stickiness can be, and as they're discovering the capabilities that technology brings for follow-up, many mistakes are being made. Again, leaders aren't asking the right questions.

It's tempting to ask, "How can we automate this?" The better question to ask is, "How do people want to experience follow-up?" The resulting experience for many unfortunate consumers is that the messages we receive don't show empathy. Smart leaders ask, "How can we automate and yet still act like human beings?"

For example, I had lunch with a business coach. We had a great meeting and discussed opportunities to potentially help one another land new clients. Several weeks later, I got a very strange email from him. It was, as I suspected, a pre-developed follow-up.

Had I not genuinely cared for his success and our potential partnership, I wouldn't have risked calling him out on the very strange, unnatural tone of his email. I told him the email message seemed a bit "off," but I was being polite. It was clear to me his franchise had told him to say these things, and I was on a list he was milking for more success. I hated being treated that way. Who wouldn't?

I followed up with this young businessman and had an honest conversation about his approach. He apologized, acknowledging the email didn't sound at all like something he'd actually say to me after our prior conversation. Hopefully, if he continues to use automation, he'll do it with greater sensitivity and consideration for his personal relationships.

This is the mantra every marketer should promote: "We'll market like real people to real people." Authentic automation provides content relevant to a client's needs or interests and is often based on the client's past behaviors. And it's usually helpful, like when you forgot to place your order on the e-commerce website, and it emailed you a reminder. I mean, who wouldn't enjoy learning about a special sale on that coffee maker Amazon knew you were thinking of purchasing?

Don't Start with Advertising, Finish with It!

Inexperienced leaders believe awareness is best created by advertising. Savvy marketing leaders know that advertising is the last idea to consider, but nonetheless a legitimate option. While advertising has never been more expensive and less effective, there is good news; it's never been more measurable. Any business considering advertising campaigns should keep this in mind and insist that all marketing spend is carefully measured and scrutinized based on its effectiveness. That might mean carefully tracking coupon use in mailers, or measuring increases in online branded search volume (searches where the brand's name is included) during a radio or billboard campaign. With selective targeting, careful scrutiny, and effective messaging, valuable advertising opportunities can be identified and employed. Even then, smart leaders consider advertising as their last resort for creating brand awareness.

CHAPTER SUMMARY

- Leaders are faced with the business challenge of creating awareness for their products or services using limited resources.

- Leaders should first discern the number of leads they need and their audiences' attitudinal segments.

- Leaders should seek to create broader awareness of their businesses by leveraging the good will they've built with their existing customers.

- Leaders should consider building referral networks with individuals and organizations that may already have connections with a target audience.

- Leaders should consider where and when consumers are making purchase decisions and build awareness strategies, advertising campaigns, and content strategies around those insights.

- Leaders should seek out and select awareness campaigns that treat consumers respectfully.

- Awareness campaigns are more effective when accompanied by a strategy to make them "sticky," for example, with retargeting, clever branding, smart messaging, and automated follow-up.

- While email automation software is useful, leaders should be on guard that the human-to-human aspect of business development is not overlooked.

QUESTION

How Do We Assemble the Right Team?

Robert was a co-founder and partner of a law practice which quickly grew to three locations in adjacent towns. The firm clearly understood the opportunity it had to grow even more, especially in its immediate community. Rather than hiring a COO, the firm decided to divide the management responsibilities among the firm's four partners. Robert had the most interest in marketing and business development, so he eagerly accepted this responsibility.

Like any good leader, Robert began his role as the firm's marketing director by taking an assessment of what they were currently doing. He realized they were using three different agencies; plus, a few of their support staff were involved with different marketing projects. One of these agencies specialized in branding. They had developed the firm's logo, letterhead, and presentation design templates. Another firm handled their digital marketing, helping their website to rank well on Google and effectively convert visitors. The third company produced video content the firm used on social media channels.

Robert knew immediately he didn't want to be communicating with three different companies. He wanted one agency for the firm, and his first order of business was to email each of these agencies, giving them 30 days' notice, per their contracts.

Robert also knew which agency he wanted to hire in their place. It was a talented creative and branding agency that served a number of large well-known brands. We'll call it Brand New 182. He had become familiar with the agency through his country club membership, where he and the agency's owner frequently played golf together.

Knowing the owner personally made Robert feel even more comfortable, and he loved the idea of using a large, established firm with a lot of credibility. He was already looking forward to the positive feedback he'd likely get from his partners. As Robert left the office that day, he said jokingly to his administrative assistant, "No one ever gets fired for hiring IBM." In other words, he was confident his partners would endorse his decision to hire a big, established marketing company in place of several local boutique agencies.

Robert met with the new agency's account executive monthly to discuss progress. He and the internal marketing committee he formed within his firm attended and reviewed each advertising campaign and approved each budget. Things seemed to be going well, and he was happy with their work.

But as the months went by, Robert started to become concerned. The firm's new business development was slowing down quarter after quarter, while other firms in their area were growing. The phones were ringing less, and they were getting fewer and fewer emails from prospective clients looking to hire them. Even their existing clients seemed to be forgetting about them, and the firm's hefty marketing budget for billboard advertising didn't seem to be helping.

What made this situation worse for Robert was seeing the firm's competitors prosper during the same period. He couldn't blame the economy or the local market for his firm's stagnation. Worse, Robert was starting to doubt his decision about firing the firm's former agencies, especially when he learned their competitors were out-pacing his firm using the same vendors he had fired and replaced a year earlier.

Robert's partners saw the decline in new business and brought it to his attention. They weren't marketing experts, but they could clearly see Robert's leadership of their firm's marketing had cost them a loss of market share, not to mention an exponential loss of future earnings. They pulled no punches reminding Robert of the situation's severity.

Leaders Simply Must Get Hiring Right

As difficult as it is to find marketing dollars in the budget and develop an effective strategy, assembling the right marketing stakeholders is equally challenging. Most leaders understand the importance of being able to find and recruit great talent, and many make a lifetime practice of getting better at it. That's why I find it so ironic most leaders I've encountered are really bad at putting the right marketing stakeholders in place.

As a representative of an agency that has been hired hundreds of times, I can testify that most leaders are quite unskilled at interviewing agencies like mine. I'm rarely asked the right questions or even hired for the right reasons. Most leaders engage with my agency because it has a good reputation for doing good work. In their minds (and mine), my agency has one of the best teams. But when it comes to marketing, the best teams don't always win. The right teams win.

Most leaders don't stop to validate whether or not we're the right team for them.

That's exactly what Robert did wrong. He believed any team as competent as Brand New 182 would turn out to be a good choice. But his agency choice had little to offer in the way of local search engine optimization, and that was a central part of the strategy Robert's firm needed.

Frankly, many of my agency's clients are in place because they knew me personally, which made them feel comfortable. While I like to think it worked out well for them, frankly, they got lucky. They truly didn't vet my agency properly. Robert also made that mistake. He relied too much on familiarity when he selected a marketing vendor and hired his golfing buddy.

Sometimes my company is passed over by prospective clients because it's not a "full-service" agency, offering a full suite of traditional media and digital marketing. I've watched these situations play out over time and observed these prospects typically underperform in business growth compared to clients who are open to using more than one agency or vendor. In today's complicated marketing landscape, agencies simply aren't good at everything. Most strategies require specific types of deep expertise and no single agency is staffed to execute every type of strategy. Smart leaders recognize this and remain open to putting together just the right mix of talent to execute the strategy they require.

For example, a small to medium-sized business may choose to work with a branding company in establishing their logo and brand standards, like the colors and fonts used across all platforms. They may engage with a digital marketing company to help them craft a digital lead generation strategy and build out digital assets aligning with the established brand standards. They may also engage with a traditional media agency for their print assets, signage, and television and radio spots in alignment with their brand standards and in coordination with their online initiatives.

There was a time when it was common for companies to name a single "agency of record." That approach is increasingly in decline as brands, large and small, are taking a more customized approach to assembling a team of marketers. Many smart businesses today consider their own diversity of abilities, take some marketing in-house, and select outside partners to access specific capabilities.

What Makes Agency Selection So Difficult?

Hiring an agency isn't easy, even for experienced leaders. There are several factors that make this especially difficult. Here are a few you might encounter as you build your teams.

Everyone sounds smart

In my city alone, there's a new agency popping up every few months. Looking at their websites, they all look smart and capable. But are they? Today, content marketing strategies are quite popular, and most agencies employ them with blogs, articles, podcasts, and instructional webinars. Everyone sounds like an expert and a thought leader, but are they actually going to get the results they talk about? Are they really that smart, or are they just busy curating and repurposing other thought leaders' content?

Experienced leaders know that not everyone who can talk about marketing can actually formulate and execute successful marketing campaigns . They look for an agency with a proven track record of working with companies similar to their own. They ask specific questions about results, budgets, and time frames. They follow up by checking references.

Everyone seems qualified

My office is within a short driving distance to Hershey, Pennsylvania. Perhaps it's proximity, but I'm sure there are dozens of marketers in my area who mention that famous brand on their list of businesses they've worked for. But what did they do exactly, and was it really effective?

When marketers claim to have worked for known brands, savvy leaders ask them specifically what they did, how long ago they did it, and who else was involved. They ask if they can get a recommendation from that client. When drilling down, leaders often come to learn that the marketer was merely part of a team engaged in a limited project for the brand. Smart leaders aren't fooled by brand name-dropping.

Salespeople sell

Most agencies are clever enough to send their brightest and best to a prospective client meeting. Leaders are far too likely to form an impression of an agency based on these polished salespeople. In fact, I've met talented presenters hired by agencies to pose as team members in order to win big accounts. Most agencies don't go this far to trick clients, but many aren't forthcoming about who will actually be working on an account once the contract is signed.

Naive leaders meet with sales teams, then pick the most impressive one. Experienced leaders insist on a peek behind the curtain. They ask who will be doing the actual work and request a meeting. They know an agency's impressive salespeople usually will have nothing to do with their own marketing outcomes. Smart leaders discuss the strategy with a prospective agency. They ask about the types of tactics that will be used and then investigate the agency's team to see if it's effectively staffed to carry out the proposed plan.

Familiarity is comfortable

Leaders tend to pick agencies the way consumers tend to select realtors. They hire the one they know or the one they run into along the way. Only later do they discover whether or not they made a good choice.

Even the most talented agencies aren't a good fit for every kind of business, size of budget, or type of strategy. Smart leaders understand the strategic play they must make, then hire a company staffed to do it and with enough success stories to prove the agency's competency.

Robert put his trust in an agency because of its well-established, solid reputation. He assumed they would be able to handle everything his company needed. He didn't take into account that even the best of agencies excel at a limited number of strategies with certain types of businesses, using specific budgets. Smart leaders are careful to search for those important details before partnering with an agency, no matter how highly it comes recommended.

Beware of industry specialists

No matter what industry a business is in, it seems there's at least one marketing company claiming to be an expert in that niche. But are they really? Yes and no. It's tempting to trust a specialist, but it's important to make sure they are truly good at their craft. Many industry specialists do have a deeper understanding of their industry, but they often dole out cookie-cutter approaches that fail to provide the customized attention businesses require to be highly successful.

For example, some years back, we were hired by a local law

firm. Prior, they were using a company that specialized in serving law firms. They had chosen that company for their law knowledge, an advantage they believed would lead to better website content. But when we copied and pasted some of the firm's website content into a search engine, it came back with some shocking results. Identical content had been published on dozens of other law firm websites by their "specialist" vendor. This duplicate content was keeping the law firm from ranking on Google's search engine. Now, years later and after giving them the customized attention they needed, the firm is enjoying top-of-page national ranking for some of their niche legal offerings, a status that continually brings new business to their door.

A templated approach would never have achieved that success. It took the careful, diligent, and persistent work of my team and theirs working together to find unique opportunities for their individual practice.

Smart leaders don't focus on the agency's specialty as much as strategy and culture alignment. Does this agency have experience in executing our strategy? Do they execute strategies for business-to-business models, big brands, packaged goods, or local service providers? Does their operational model align with what we require? Will our people work well with theirs? Have they done great work for other clients with a marketing budget similar to ours?

Asking the Right Questions

Having been at the receiving end of both good and bad questions for more than a decade with hundreds of businesses, I believe I've seen the best and worst approaches at interviewing agencies. I've become accustomed to the most common bad question: "What would you guys do for my company, and how much would it cost?" Obviously, they're assuming we are an agency with "tactics-for-sale," and their strategy is "tactical trial and error." They are there to learn which tactics we are promoting and how much we charge for them.

When we're asked this question, we turn the tables by asking our own questions. "Why are you here? What's the business case for you to spend money on marketing? What are the financial drivers of your business, and what are the opportunities for growth in your industry? What do you perceive to be the marketing problems your company is having? What is the lifetime value of acquiring a new customer?" We act like partners, even before we're hired. We do that because in the end, we're seeking partnership, and we'd like any potential client to get a taste of it. We are not alone in that approach. Other good agencies also engage prospective clients with these types of questions. Smart leaders are wary of an agency that simply plays the role of an "order-taker," rather than challenging their thinking or bringing new insights into the conversation.

What strategy do you recommend?

Leaders can uncover important information about an agency's qualifications by asking good questions. I suggest, "What strategies have you used in industries similar to mine?" Or ask, "Given what you know about my company, what type of overarching strategy would you suggest we consider?"

If a leader is trying to hire an agency for ongoing partnership, they should observe how naturally that prospective company engages in these conversations. If they use your time to sell the merits of their preferred tactics, that might be a signal to walk away, especially if those tactics aren't connected to a measurable over-arching strategy. The conversation you want to hear is one that centers around your uniqueness, not the agency's.

Who on your team would be executing that strategy?

In my experience, this is an important peek behind the curtain, and leaders almost never ask for it. Any credible agency will have no trouble talking about the team that will come together to bring great results. Low-caliber agencies will struggle with this question. Why? Because they aren't really staffed to execute the plan they're pitching. They may be outsourcing much of the work, even to third-world countries for ten cents on the dollar. They may have only one team member to do all of the digital marketing work they are proposing.

It may be of little consequence to a leader if agency work is outsourced, but wise leaders audit and assess if adequate resources are truly in place to fulfill the work, or if the potential contract would be the agency's funding source for hiring new staff.

Can you please describe your process and show me some work samples?

On the other hand, if a leader is hiring an agency for a specific project, a stronger focus should be placed on the agency's process and whether or not they seem experienced and organized. They should meet with the account executive they would be assigned to.

Leaders hiring talent for a creative project should ask to see the specific work of the designer or designers who would be assigned to the project. They should focus on whether or not the designer has, in the past, delivered the design style that aligns with their brand and appeals to your audience.

What budget do you work with?

Some time back, I engaged in an agency interview with one of our clients considering a very large and specialized company to launch a new initiative. We were impressed with the company's capabilities. But when I asked about their typical client's budget, we found the information we needed to make our decision. They mostly served clients with budgets five times that of our proposed amount. We knew they wouldn't be a good fit for us.

Experienced leaders come to an agency with a realistic budget in mind. With that number, they ask the prospective agency what budgets they are most comfortable serving. Every agency has their range that best aligns with their operational model. Asking the agency to work with a higher or lower budget than what falls within their sweet spot typically brings less-than-optimal results. Smart leaders find agencies that align with their budget.

Does this agency sell storage sheds or gardens?

When someone is shopping for a storage shed for their back-yard, they decide how big it should be, the look and style they prefer, and the quality and price they're comfortable with. Some aspects of marketing involve finite deliverables, like a logo, a brand standards document, or a 30-second TV commercial. When a company needs to rebrand itself, create a magazine or print media campaign, launch billboards, run radio spots, create and run a TV commercial, or send mailers, it will be well-served to find an agency that is good at this. This is shed-buying. It's a finite deliverable.

Contrast shed-buying with planting a backyard garden, which involves planning, planting, and then ongoing maintenance. Many aspects of marketing are ongoing commitments, especially online marketing objectives like maintaining a ranking on search engines, executing an ongoing content strategy, improving a website's con-version performance over time, or managing online reputation. Those initiatives require continuous attention and iterative improvement.

Leaders should think about their marketing needs. Do they need a shed-seller or a gardener? Many companies need both, but most agencies are better at one than the other.

When a business leader is looking for a gardener-type agency, even greater emphasis should be placed on the potential for good partnership. They should ask questions like, "How often will we meet to discuss our progress? Will we be receiving monthly reports? What will be covered in those reports?"

As mentioned earlier, it will be valuable to understand the agency's culture, values, and personality and consider if these are a good fit. All of these factors, along with typical client retention, are predictors of whether this agency is good at being a partner. Partnership is a key element in hiring a "gardener" agency.

But when a business is more concerned about having some creative work done, like a brochure, a billboard campaign, or a logo redesign, other attributes should be the focus. For example, the quality and type of workmanship is of central importance. It's imperative to look at other work the agency has done utilizing their existing staff to evaluate whether the agency is a good fit. Do your best to determine if the candidate agency has experience in the type of design, look, and feel your company needs and that they do quality work.

Had Robert been guided by this advice, he might have asked very different questions when choosing agency partners. He would have insisted on having discussions about strategy to get greater clarity on what would be needed. He would have also better assessed the agency's in-house talent and track record to see if it aligned with the needs of his firm.

Putting the right marketing team in place is one of the most important tasks of the business leader and is the primary factor in predicting marketing success. That said, many leaders limit their marketing success by simply hiring a familiar agency or one with a "big name."

Hiring the Right In-house Marketers

As businesses grow, marketing needs and the complexity of executing them do as well. Leaders often don't have the time or mental bandwidth to be involved in meeting with agencies, reviewing reports, and other time-consuming tasks. It makes sense to hire a director of marketing. Sometimes a company has repetitive marketing responsibilities easily handled by lower-skilled team members. It might make sense to take those tasks in-house, delegating them to an existing team member or hiring someone new.

In my experience, the most successful model is a mix of in-house marketers and highly skilled outsourced workers, usually from an agency. This model seems to work for small and medium-sized businesses as well as larger brands. But hiring in-house marketers is typically easier to do wrong than right, especially for leaders who haven't done it before. Here are some guiding principles.

Deciding what to outsource

As a business grows, leaders are often faced with the issue of increased staffing for their marketing needs. Should they hire employees for this or contract with a third party? Some leaders have a strong desire to keep this responsibility in-house, avoiding the high cost of agency fees. Others prefer to outsource marketing entirely so their business can focus solely on its core profitable activities. But who's right?

Actually, every situation is different depending on the industry, factors related to competition, and the specific needs of the business.

There are guiding principles, however, that will guide a leader through this decision. Leaders should outsource marketing responsibilities that involve these four things.

Rare talent

There are many graphic designers, but relatively few truly gifted ones. The difference between "good-enough" work and great work may not seem significant to a naive leader, but the difference in results could be dramatic. When you experience the "sticker shock" of hiring rare talent, just remember, only bad marketing is expensive. Rare talent is typically found within agencies who build their businesses around the value these gifted individuals bring.

Deep expertise

Some skills can only be mastered after years of experience and a lot of success and failure. Conversion optimization, the ability to organize information on a webpage so visitors take the desired action, is one of those. Brand strategy, reputation management, and strategy development are also on this list.

Fast-changing technologies

Do you think your marketing person is an SEO expert? Unless they're spending 25 percent of their work days reading, attending conferences, and staying involved in the SEO community's conversations, they're probably years behind, and that's a disadvantage your competition could certainly exploit. Any technology that changes fast will require a commitment to keeping your in-house team member up-to-speed. If SEO is an important part of your marketing strategy, in the long run, you're better off hiring outside resources for these needs.

Marketing teamwork

Interactive media have made most marketing efforts more complex. Even a simple ad campaign may require a web developer, paid search expert, designer, copywriter, and strategist. Even experienced agencies find it extremely difficult to recruit and retain their digital marketing teams. In most cases, it doesn't make sense for a small business to ask one person to do it all, or to build an in-house team. When teamwork is required, consider outsourcing.

Deciding what to keep in-house

While outsourcing provides access to individuals with rare talent, it often comes at a high price. It may make sense to assign some marketing responsibilities to in-house employees to save money and have those tasks more "closely held." For example, if a business is constantly communicating with an audience, the hours spent doing this can get quite expensive at agency rates and an in-house employee may have easier access to company messages and information. Regular communications and a few other categories of marketing tasks can sometimes be performed cheaper and more efficiently by employees. Here are some other examples.

Repetitive tasks

With the rise of interactive media, consumers have higher expectations than ever for on-demand communication. When they post something on social media that relates to an experience they've had with a company, or when they ask a question online, consumers expect a quick response. They expect a business's online presence to be kept up to date, whether it's holiday hours, specials, or new offerings. All of these new business responsibilities require manpower, and many businesses are covering these responsibilities using existing employees or by creating new positions.

Content generation

With the rise of digital media, many small businesses need to generate more content than ever for website updates, blogs, podcasts, social media, and video channels. While a degree of expertise is required, repetitive tasks like posts on social media, basic website updates, and requests for online reviews, can often be performed in-house. Some (but probably not all) video content can be created by employees, along with informal photography and simple posts and updates on social media.

Marketing coordination

Today more than ever, businesses are using more than one marketing vendor, each chosen for their specific expertise. Managing multiple relationships requires coordination. In times past, one agency was commonly classified as the agency of record, a status that often allowed them to play this role. But today, many businesses have stopped granting that title to any one vendor. That means someone, typically a company's employee, needs to coordinate multiple relationships.

Common Mistakes Leaders Make in Hiring

If you spend more than a decade watching how business leaders make good and bad hiring choices, you'll notice certain patterns. Here are some common mistakes I've observed leaders make in building internal marketing teams. By looking carefully over this list, you might be able to avoid making them.

Task-oriented

As leaders build an in-house team to perform repetitive tasks, they'll likely encounter a pervasive and insidious attitude. They'll find their team members believe marketing is easy, and successful marketing simply involves getting a list of tasks done and incorporating best practices along the way. They become task-oriented, and as such, neglect to be guided by strategy. As a generation of tech-savvy employees enter the workforce, this attitude is becoming increasingly pervasive. Smart leaders know that while marketing may seem easy, *good marketing is difficult* and hard to achieve.

Non-strategic

Based on my local banking experiences, tellers have some opinions on how a bank should be run. While that input is valuable and should be heard by the bank's leaders, a bank should never be run by the tellers. Higher-level thinking is required, as are insights not typically on a teller's radar. Likewise, task-oriented in-house marketing team members have some valuable ideas to contribute. But as a leader, you need to resist their desire to take the lead. In addition to their input, you should involve strategic thinkers outside your organization to influence your decisions. But don't get a lot of different opinions. Seek out just a few from successful marketing experts.

Self-reporting

Many leaders hire in-house teams, then allow those individuals to self-report on their marketing success. I once saw a cartoon where a marketing team was in front of a board of directors with a flip chart. The chart said, "We did an awesome job this month because we loved our work." Leaders must remain diligent in establishing and maintaining an independent review of their marketing effectiveness. In-house marketing teams are often eager to take this responsibility off the hands of the naive leader and craft their own reports. Smart leaders don't allow it.

Behind the times

I just attended a conference where I learned about a new initiative in Google's search engine that will open the door for many of our clients to significantly increase their leads this year. I'm sure none of our clients' competitors know about this, unless they use an aggressive agency that is staying up-to-date and obtaining first-to-know information. Leaders that rely on small in-house teams, in my experience, fall behind the times. Staying up-to-date is yet another reason I believe the ideal solution for most businesses is to have a mix of in-house and outsourced marketing stakeholders.

Blind spots

You don't know what you don't know. That's true for you as a leader, but it's also true for your small in-house team. By involving a mix of in-house and outsourced marketing team members, you're much more likely to expose your blind spots, aspects of marketing you may be neglecting or performing poorly.

Failing with Frugality

Tim was destined to be self-employed. Right out of college, he started his own painting company out of his garage and soon grew to nine full-time employees. The money he saved by working out of his home made it possible to underprice his competition and quickly gain market share in his area.

Just as Tim easily started his business, other new competitors were doing the same, and they were poaching his customers. His company's growth flattened. Tim knew it was time to step up his marketing game, but this was new territory for him.

Tim's guiding mantra had always been to spend as little money as possible. He defaulted to this approach in his marketing initiative, and after finding out the hourly rate of marketing agencies in his area, he decided to instead hire an in-house, part-time marketing assistant, Jane. Jane was a talented artist and had recently graduated at the top of her class from a local design school. Tim was delighted to have her and even more pleased her pay rate was about one-quarter of what an agency would have charged him.

Jane's first task was to bring the company's website up to date and get it ranked on Google. Jane was generally familiar with her boss's request, so she didn't object to taking on the assignment. She had taken a class on this type of work in school.

But by the following year, Tim was frustrated. The website looked better than ever thanks to Jane's work, but they had actually dropped in their ranking on Google and were getting fewer leads. Meanwhile, several smaller, less-established local competitors were out-ranking Tim on search engines and turned up everywhere online.

Looking at his sales projections, Tim estimated he was more than $500,000 behind where he'd hoped to be by now. Had he made the right decision by hiring Jane?

Many leaders choke on the idea of paying outsourced experts high amounts for specialty services like SEO. Regularly, I observe leaders struggling to understand which types of marketing services to bring in-house and which to outsource to vendors. In an effort to cut costs, leaders make poor decisions in this regard, and over time, those choices cost their organizations a lot of money in lost opportunity.

In my experience, the way some leaders move their marketing in-house often hurts them. In-house team members don't have the peer stimulation, ongoing development resources, or diversity of talent to help compensate for their limited expertise. In-house marketing staff tend to gravitate toward activities and strategies they're most comfortable with, not necessarily what their business really needs. They're often expected to develop a strategy while their talents lie with designing, writing, or programming.

Sometimes leaders confuse a marketing platform acumen with competency in marketing. For example, just because a college grad-uate grew up with Facebook and Instagram doesn't mean they'll know how to wield those communication platforms to help your business grow.

Hiring the Swiss Army Knife

Several companies and organizations have reached out to me asking for my help in hiring in-house marketing employees. Without exception, each was well on their way toward making the same mis-take. They were trying to hire a human version of a marketing swiss army knife.

They wanted someone with a good design sense and competency in popular design software. The candidate needed excellent written and verbal communication skills. They needed to be savvy with social media and able to think strategically. The candidate would be responsible for doing website updates, emailing newsletters, handling internal communications, designing brochures and advertisements, doing SEO, and they would be familiar with Google Analytics software. Worse, the business was expecting to compensate this marketing unicorn with a middle-class salary.

At the time of writing this book, marketers with skills in SEO, conversion, user experience, and paid search were hard to find. When leaders want to bring all of these tactics in-house, they fail to realize how nearly impossible it is to stay current in multiple areas. My company's team of digital marketers spends almost 25 percent of their time studying, learning, experimenting, reading, and attending educational webinars and conferences in their single category of expertise. They're constantly learning from one another as well, a peer stimulation that is extremely important. We often joke that in our industry, we go to bed smart, but wake up stupid.

In any type of work where deep expertise is required and areas of it are constantly changing, I advise leaders to use outsourced partners. A qualified partner will bring the diversity of skills needed to execute strategy, ongoing learning and advisement, and affordable access to multiple software-as-a-service tools used in digital marketing.

The Best In-House Models

There is one model I've seen work consistently across all industries and businesses of all sizes. Leaders will get the best

marketing results by hiring in-house marketers who not only understand marketing, but are also highly skilled at managing people.
Leaders who seek out and hire for those attributes, and provide an
adequate budget for marketing and outsourcing, will typically find
success.

Unfortunately, marketing staff are usually hired for their
marketing skills, not their management capabilities. These in-house
marketers sometimes feel threatened by the idea of using outsourced
talent, especially if it's well beyond their own. They keep work
in-house that should be outsourced to professionals, and they often
get involved in minutiae and details they should be delegating. In the
end, they sabotage strategic vendor relationships. I've seen this play
out several times within my own agency. Twice in our recent past,
we've needed to fire clients because their in-house marketing
employee made serving them an impossible task for my team.

Sometimes the opposite happens. Companies hire a young,
tech-savvy marketing leader who believes in the now-popular misconception that "marketing is easy." They believe it's really just
about getting stuff done, blogs published, Google Ads run, social
media updated. They don't value the strategic vision outside marketing resources bring, and they treat these resources like easy-to-
replace vendors.

Smart leaders delegate marketing responsibilities to good managers who understand marketing. Especially for the first marketing
employee a business hires, the priority consideration should be
whether the candidate is good at working with people, is humble,
and is able to see the bigger picture while managing details. Seeking
to take marketing totally in-house for a small business is often a formula for marketing mediocrity.

Putting too many eggs in one basket

A few years back, one of my clients spoke with me about how their online paid campaigns were burning through cash. The company they had hired used a "set it and forget it" approach to their campaigns, and the performance showed it. My client decided taking this in-house would be prudent.

My team agreed to train a candidate on their team to manage these campaigns, a complicated responsibility. It took us the better part of a year, and even then, our regular assistance was needed. Then the unthinkable happened. She quit and took a different job with another company. My client was back to square one as she was the only one in their organization who had these rare skills and expensive education.

For long-term, ongoing responsibilities that are high-stakes and require unique skills and extensive education, leaders will be in a safer position if they rely on an agency, especially an agency with a redundancy of talent.

The solopreneur

I've worked with many clients over the years who had hired outside, one-person agencies to complete tasks, typically for building cheap websites. They find these talented individuals through their personal networks or on work-for-hire websites. However, when these vendors move on, they leave the clients in dire straits. I've encountered many alarming situations like this when clients have been unable to access their websites, manage their company's domain names, or access important passwords to online assets after their one-man agency became unreachable without warning. Smart leaders avoid building marketing dependency on a single person.

Rather, they look for longer-term, sustainable partnerships.

Whether outsourced or in-house, a team of one is not a good solution for serving a company's marketing needs. Not only does it create a single point of vulnerability, it puts unrealistic expectations on one employee to be a jack-of-all-trades.

Businesses too often attempt to hire a multi-talented marketer when hiring their first in-house marketing team member. Smart leaders, however, prioritize the new hire's ability to manage other people, vendors, and agencies. They understand their ongoing need to outsource to multiple vendors to get the deep expertise they require. The persona they look for in a marketing director is someone especially good at coordinating all the stakeholders and processes.

Affordable talent

I once talked to a prospective client who desperately needed help with his marketing but hadn't budgeted properly for taking his product to market. In that discussion, he mentioned he could have a brochure made in a developing country for one-fifth the price. I encouraged him to consider the quality of the work. Marketing is only as valuable as the success it creates. Poor marketing has no value. In fact, it can actually damage a brand by giving consumers the wrong impression.

That's why talented marketers are able to command good prices for their work. And it's also why they're able to turn away business, even when they're more expensive than their competition. If any marketing effort is worth doing, it's worth doing right. Smart leaders don't shop for the cheapest talent trying to find some undiscovered person who will work for an intern's wage. Instead, smart leaders look for quality execution. In the end, only great marketing has great value.

At the beginning of this chapter, we discussed Robert's failure to hire the right agency and the eventual loss this caused to his company. If he'd had more experience coming into this role, what could he have done differently?

Most likely, he would have ignored the need he felt to have just one consolidated agency. He would have prioritized the local digital strategy his firm needed and would have sought out an agency qualified to execute it. He would have asked prospective agencies if they'd done similar work in the past and whether they were staffed well enough to perform his needed tactics. He might have hired another in-house team member to coordinate marketing efforts, taking this responsibility off his own shoulders and into the hands of someone who understands marketing strategy.

Armed with these few insights and positioned to ask the right questions, Robert would have led his company into a prosperous outcome. The same is true for any leader as they assemble winning marketing teams.

CHAPTER SUMMARY

- Leaders have the important and difficult job of assembling the right team of marketing stakeholders, often a mix of agency partners and in-house employees.

- A "right-fit" agency can be identified by asking questions related to their typical client budget, industry vertical experience, most-used strategies, and staffing. Leaders should discern if an agency is more comfortable to perform traditional marketing campaigns or interactive strategies.

- Smart leaders outsource tasks requiring rare talent or deep expertise, along with ones that involve fast-changing technologies or skilled teamwork. Other marketing responsibilities, such as repetitive tasks, content creation, and marketing coordination, are best performed in-house by employees.

- Leaders should use caution when managing in-house marketing teams that may become more tactical than strategic, or work without third party oversight.

- Leaders shouldn't always be guided solely by cost in making agency choices or hiring decisions, and should keep realistic expectations about any one marketing employee's capabilities.

How Can We Bring Out the Best in Our Marketing Teams?

Like any relationship, the ongoing success between a business and an agency involves the right behaviors from all parties. But working with an agency and overseeing marketing directors can be challenging, especially for leaders who don't feel confident in this area. Leaders often fail to realize just how much their behavior impacts a hired agency's ability to perform. Sadly, the worst behaviors come out in leaders in the midst of a high-stakes project, like in the middle of a website or custom application build-out. Consider this short story about a leader named Charles and the problems his decisions and behavior created.

A Tale of Two Assistants

Charles knew it was time to update his eight-year-old website. He recognized the importance of his company's online presence for getting new business, and he also saw how he had fallen behind his competition.

He hired what he believed to be the right company. They weren't the cheapest, but they were a good fit for his business and were very talented. Charles personally oversaw and reviewed the contract with his new agency and attended the kick-off meeting. Though he had a lot of other responsibilities related to running the company, he prioritized this work, taking time out to make sure the project got off to a good start.

It was important to Charles that he ended up with a fantastic website, one that would be the envy of his competitors. Charles drove a bright red Porsche 911 he had recently inherited. He liked how he felt when he drove the car, and if he was honest with himself, that's how he wanted to feel about his website. He wanted the "wow factor," the kind of look and feel that made others a bit jealous.

Admittedly, Charles felt a bit uneasy about directing this process. He had very little experience with website-building and virtually no training in design or user experience architecture. One month into the process, when his agency presented the first version of the homepage design for his approval, he felt he should involve Mary, his administrative assistant, and Elizabeth, his bookkeeper. Mary in particular had more experience since she had been involved in the company's last website design.

Mary had been with the company for two decades. In fact, she was the administrative assistant for Charles' mother when she had been the CEO. Elizabeth was much younger, and Charles admired her technical prowess. Whenever he had an issue with his computer or with using a website, Elizabeth was there to help him.

Both employees had a keen interest in this website project, but prior to this meeting, they hadn't been involved or included in conversations. Because they didn't trust Charles to lead this process, they were especially pleased to be invited to the design review. In fact, both of them had just read a book about marketing, and one of the chapters outlined some excellent advice they were eager to implement.

Daryl, from the agency, did a great job of presenting his design work, explaining how it aligned with their brand and the stated business objectives. He reminded them of the audiences the website would serve, pointed out how it aligned with their brand standards, and explained how the design supported the stated user experience objectives. When they were finished, there was an uncomfortable silence in the room.

Elizabeth and Mary turned and made eye contact with one another as if to communicate, "I bet I know what you're thinking," or, "I'm so dissatisfied with this, I don't even know where to begin."

Charles broke the silence. "It's nice," he said in a way that made it clear the criticism was about to follow. "It's just not what I expected. I had hoped for a bit more." He paused for an awkwardly long time, so Daryl helped him finish his sentence.

"Let me guess, you want to say, 'It just doesn't pop,'" Daryl suggested.

"Exactly!" Charles said, seeming a bit more relaxed now that Daryl understood how he felt. "That's exactly what I was trying to say."

"We hear that a lot," Daryl said, half out loud, half under his breath.

With the ice now broken, Elizabeth and Mary were ready to condescend. "I don't think you really understand at all what we're looking for," Mary started. "This isn't even close," she said as she pushed her laptop a few inches away from her to demonstrate her revulsion.

Young Elizabeth took courage from her teammates and weighed in. "We were hoping for a moving banner or even a movie-type header, like the other good websites all have now. And we'd like to see more effects as you scroll down, you know, like when things slide in from the side."

Mary jumped in before Elizabeth had even finished. "And I can think of at least five things that need to be on this home page that aren't here. For example, there's not very much information here for our existing clients or for recruiting new employees. This whole design caters to potential new clients."

Daryl, still keeping his composure, remarked, "I understand, Elizabeth, but Charles and I discussed this at length earlier in this process, and he signed off on the idea that we'd prioritize new first-time buyers."

"Well, we'll have a discussion about that internally and get back to you," Mary said as she organized her things, signaling she felt the meeting was over. It had become clear to Daryl that Mary was really running the show now, and that Charles' lack of confidence about design and websites had made him a different leader than Daryl had first thought.

"Why don't you put together some other concepts and run them by us by, say, next week?" Mary said. "We'll see if you're getting any closer."

Daryl left the meeting feeling very frustrated. He believed he and his team had been treated unfairly. On the way home, he called Charles, who picked up immediately.

"I was caught a bit off guard by how the meeting went today," confessed Daryl. "I thought we were on track with our process, and everyone was on the same page. But now I feel like we have to go back to the beginning and have every conversation all over again with Elizabeth and Mary in the room."

"Well, I believe in allowing my team to have a say in these things, and Elizabeth and Mary are better with this marketing stuff than I am." Charles explained. "I'm not going to force a new website down their throats. We'll just need to be patient and allow them to weigh in. Besides, I was really disappointed in the design you presented. It just didn't move me like I wanted it to."

Daryl was glad he was driving and not in the room. He pulled over because at this point, his hands were shaking. Daryl had more than a decade of experience in designing high-performing websites. In fact, he was a highly celebrated designer with more awards under his belt than any professional in the region. But more than that, he worked with a team that made high-performing websites, ones with conversion rates that out-performed the industry standard by large margins. He and his team not only knew how to make high-performing websites, they were very confident this one was a real winner.

Daryl had started out making a website to achieve a business goal. He built it to reinforce the company's brand and to influence and convert customers who might visit the site. But now his assignment had changed. Now, Daryl's assignment was to build a website for this newly formed committee, and each member's opinions and tastes would need to be drawn out and implemented.

"I understand," Daryl replied.

"I know you tried, and don't worry, we're not giving up on you just yet," Charles said patronizingly. "I'll meet with Elizabeth and Mary, and we'll get back to you with a list of things you should change."

"You do know this will take us out-of-scope with our budget, don't you?" Daryl asked. "We already had extensive conversations about what you wanted in a website, but now you're asking us to have those same conversations over again."

Daryl could hear some background noise in the room, and he could tell that he no longer had Charles' undivided attention.

"I know in some ways, this is a little unfair to you, but that's just how it goes sometimes, and I expect you to honor your contract," Charles replied.

He went on to tell Daryl a story of how a client had made unfair demands on them last year, and how his team had stayed until 11 p.m. for three nights and had come through for the client. "That's just what good companies do," Charles lectured.

Daryl wasn't new to this sort of situation, and neither were his teammates. They understood they could insist on a change of work order and getting paid more money, which would likely end the relationship, or they could become order-takers and do their best to get the site launched, taking a loss on this project, a sacrifice worth having this nightmare go away.

Daryl knew every bit of progress he had made toward building a well-performing website was now of no benefit. He knew his company would make no profit on this project, either because of cost overruns, or because Charles would fire them. He knew from experience his new assignment was to discern what would impress the company's newly-formed committee, and to build something to satisfy them as quickly as possible. Worse, Daryl knew the eventual product would not perform as well as the design right in front of them.

In the coming weeks, they went through three more rounds of design revisions. Daryl refrained from giving them any advice. While Charles, Mary, and Elizabeth didn't agree with one another, Daryl incorporated some suggestions from each of them and was able to launch the new website, two months behind schedule.

Daryl was not surprised a month later when he got a call from Charles. "I hate to say anything, but this website you built for us is not performing well at all," he said. Daryl was not surprised by this call. He already knew from looking at the website's user data that visitors weren't staying on the site or converting. He knew that subsequently, their ranking had dropped on Google's search results, and fewer people were finding the website. Elizabeth had written a scathing review about him and his agency on both Yelp and Google, complaining that Daryl launched the website two months late and that Daryl "just doesn't get it," referring to the three rounds of revisions it took for him to figure out what would satisfy their committee of critics.

Everyone Loses

Sadly, each aspect of this story happens every day to agencies and to companies. There's a little bit of Charles in many leaders today, and agencies get a front row seat to observe organizational dysfunction. Everyone loses when leaders don't manage the strategic relationships their teams have with vendors, especially creatives. Enormous opportunities are missed.

In this case, Charles had a responsibility to stay the course with the agency's process. *Each stakeholder should have been involved in the process from the beginning.* All feedback from within his organization should have been given to him to filter and pass on, only if relevant. Charles or someone assigned from the beginning should have been the single liaison with Daryl.

While Charles had every right to demand results, he was foolish to trust his own or his team's design feedback over that of a professional. He would have been entitled to demand the site be corrected after launch if agreed-upon performance metrics weren't met, but he was foolish for getting too involved in the details of how to reach them. Smart leaders never micro-manage the artist's paintbrush.

When agencies see that the only way to fulfill a contract is to allow a customer to be in control of each decision and process, they stop bringing insights. To survive, they shift from caring about a good product to caring about closure. They shift from doing what they know is best to doing what the customer thinks is best. In the end, everyone loses. Smart leaders don't do that to their vendors.

Design By Committee

What's the definition of a camel? It's a horse designed by a committee. The best ideas aren't led by consensus, they're led by talented individuals empowered to make decisions. When it comes to design decisions, however, far too many individuals feel qualified to influence outcomes. If something doesn't align with their expectations and their specific tastes, they're confident it's wrong and must be changed.

This puts inexperienced leaders in an awkward situation. On the one hand, they want buy-in from their teams. They may even want help evaluating whether a hired expert is truly on track in many important respects. But unintentionally, they allow an impromptu internal design committee to micromanage the creative process and direct experienced design professionals.

Smart leaders see this coming. They're clear about the input desired from each stakeholder they involve from their organizations and how that feedback will be used. Design by committee is the most common problem leaders will experience as their internal teams work with external vendors. Smart leaders prevent that from occurring, and for good reason. While they may ask for the opinion of others they trust, they or someone they appoint are the single liaison, point of contact, and filtering voice that communicates with the creative talent.

Search any art museum and try to find a brilliant piece of work made by a committee. You won't find one. Wise leaders never allow a committee to oversee creativity. When they do so, they're empowering everyone to say "no" and no one to say "yes." When you create something that everyone approves of, no one will love it. When multiple people are asked for feedback on creative work, it's crucial the leader keeps it reined in to specific commentary that's as objective as possible. For example, is it following brand standards? Does it align with the creative brief established at the beginning of the process? Is it designed for the intended audience(s)? In essence, the marketing leader should think of themselves as the museum curator, not an art coach. They should stick to the question, "Does this belong in our museum?"

Giving feedback to artists can be stressful for everyone. Creative workers are notorious for taking personal offense from any suggestions or criticisms about their work. But tactful leaders begin by acknowledging the positive steps that have been made and what they like about the work, instead of diving right into what they want changed. When addressing items to change, it's important to attach remarks to overarching goals that were agreed upon in advance. Which audience are we designing for? Does this create the right impression right away, align with our brand essence, and communicate our differentiation? Does this provide the right experience for our intended audience?

For example, "This proposed design communicates professionalism, an attribute we value in our law firm. At the same time, many of the pictures and the design in general seem very corporate. We don't really have that feel in our office, and in fact, many of our clients are small business owners, and many are farmers. How might we make this design make that sector of our clientele recognize we're a good fit for them?"

In another case, an effective leader might say, "I've seen your other work, and I don't believe the work you've shown me measures up to that. I don't want to be in a position to tell you how to make this design better, but I'd like to know if you feel this is the best you have to offer." A good designer will defend their work, and you need to hear that argument. If you truly were served second-rate work, most discerning creatives will admit a design needs more attention, especially if addressed respectfully.

It's very tempting for leaders and those they involve in creative review to insert their personal perspectives as though they're the intended audience. They count their own reactions as strong evidence that change is needed. I've seen many great websites brought down in quality because people in power demanded the website be changed to appeal to their personal tastes rather than the website's intended audience.

Respect the Process

Building websites and other complex marketing campaigns involves many steps and requires adherence to processes. Any agency worth hiring has deep expertise in using successful processes to keep things on track and on budget, and to ensure a positive outcome and a good experience along the way.

Smart leaders ask a lot of questions about an agency's process before hiring them. It's an effective way to know in advance if an agency is set to deliver what they promise. But effective leaders take it a step further. They're careful to honor and respect the process.

In preparing to write this book, I surveyed agencies across the country, asking them about their experiences working with companies. The number one issue they brought up was no surprise to me. Business leaders who respect the agency's process arrive at great outcomes; those who don't create chaos, frustration, budget overruns, and poor outcomes.

Respect the Timeline

The biggest complaint agencies have, and the most typical manner in which leaders hurt their organization's marketing, is this: distraction. When leaders are focusing on other things, they aren't responsive. They miss deadlines. They disrupt their marketer's productivity timelines. Leaders who don't delegate well turn themselves into organizational bottlenecks. These top-down leaders are the worst types for marketing teams to serve.

For example, this year, a client who for years had been extremely happy with our work put another team member in charge of managing their new website build. The new delegate got busy with other things and wouldn't respond to us with design approvals, content review, or photography feedback. We had reserved our programmers' calendars to build this website once the design and content assets were approved. But the client changed his own internal priorities, didn't communicate with us, and then lied, complaining to his boss that we were holding things up.

It was infuriating. Months later, when we got design approval and were ready to go into production, our web developers' production schedules were booked. The client was furious because we didn't immediately stop production on other clients' websites to do theirs. They reminded us of our original deadline. They bludgeoned us with lectures about good customer service.

We listened, did our best to finish the website as soon as we could, then fired the client. Good agencies won't allow their teams to be demoralized, overworked, or insulted. Smart leaders know the value of having a talented agency energized to do great work on their behalf, and they do their part to maintain that crucial partnership.

When we have a client who carefully looks at our schedule and remarks, "I'll have to make sure my sales team will have some time next month to give you the input you'll need to build out this content," we know things are looking positive. Or when we hear, "How can I support you in keeping this project on track?" we know we'll be able to exceed the leader's expectations. They're respecting our proven process which, in turn, will bring them great results.

Include Each Stakeholder from the Beginning

One important way to honor an agency's or vendor's process is to keep the members of the team consistent. When leaders allow a new stakeholder to be added mid-process, they do everyone a huge disservice. Sometimes it's necessary because of changes in staffing. When it's unavoidable, leaders should give fair attention to the impact and disruption it's likely to cause and make adjustments to time and budget expectations. Leaders should be careful to bring everyone who will have a voice in the website's development into the process from the start.

Build a Sports Car

Many leaders fall into the trap of evaluating their website based on how much it feels like a status symbol. They want something with stunning design and the latest and fanciest animation features. They think their customers will be impressed by that. They're wrong.

Website visitors are more impressed with a site's usefulness than its flashiness. Is the navigation intuitive to use? Can they easily find the information they're looking for? Many leaders want their website analogous to a status-gaining, head-turning sports car. But their users want a practical, easy-to-drive minivan. Wise leaders don't let vanity get in the way. They focus on their customers' experiences by asking these questions:

1. Who's coming to this website?
2. What's on their mind?
3. What should their first impression be?
4. What do they need to learn or experience?
5. What do we hope they'll do before they leave?

Experienced designers understand how to build that type of website. It may not be exactly what a leader first expects. Rather than micromanaging the design work, smart leaders set performance objectives in advance, and after launch, hold the website builders accountable for the design's performance.

Make It Perfect—Later

Inexperienced leaders allow their organizations to agonize over whether or not a website is ready to launch. More and more, small revisions are requested and months are lost in developing the perfect website.

If there's one thing I've learned over the years in helping develop websites, it's this: you can't develop a perfect website before you launch it. That's because you can never completely predict how people will use a website or navigate through its pages.

Great websites are launched early, after basic content is right and proofreaders have had their turn. Then, with the careful discipline of observing how users navigate the website, incremental changes are made. In time and with incremental improvements, the website evolves into a high-performing marketing tool. Even using the best user-experience design principles, the ultimate websites are always built over numerous iterations refined by using data, not subjective opinions.

That's why experienced leaders and teams allow a new website to go live much sooner than inexperienced ones do. Often the greatest insights are gained the first months after launch, not during an overly-extended phase of fine-tooth-combing and feature-adding before they go live. Wise leaders launch quickly and evolve constantly.

Respect the People

I know the client-agency relationship has gone bad when my creative directors are being told what to design by the client. Given the high skill level, education, and extensive experience of my team, when someone who has never built a website is instructing them on how to design web layout, we've crossed a line. Unfortunately, that line gets crossed a lot, and leaders allow it.

When a business does the hard work of selecting a talented agency, and they've discussed the brand standards, the target audience, and many other specific directives, they need to trust the true experts and resist the temptation to become a design coach. While it's tempting to suddenly shift to using personal taste when giving feedback on design, it's a dangerous path that typically leads to a sub-standard outcome. When you hire professionals, you have two choices—trust them or fire them.

Smart leaders and their teams demand alignment with stated design objectives and with the business case for any marketing spend. But they shouldn't ever try to direct the pen of the artist.

Four Behaviors that Will Revolutionize Outcomes

Recently, I met with my leadership team to discuss our company's direction. We took a close look at the types of clients that, over time, found marketing success from our work. While we saw patterns in industry types, even more obvious was the strong correlation between leader behaviors and marketing outcomes. We identified these four attributes of good leaders, the ones that brought out the best in us.

"Getting" the vision

When leaders understand the business case for their marketing budget, the strategy they're using, and how the metrics for evaluating progress relate to both of these, we're able to have the right conversations and stay on track to produce great results over time. But when leaders don't understand the big picture, they get sidetracked on vanity metrics like, for example, how many people are following them on Twitter. Leaders without clarity ask the wrong questions, focus on the wrong things, and have trouble justifying the value of their marketing spend. In turn, the agency they've partnered with spends a disproportionate amount of time managing the client, leaving less time to work toward the client's success.

Trusting the agency to do good work

So much marketing today involves digital platforms as part of any campaign, and those platforms are measurable. There's never been an easier time for leaders to trust their marketing partners while still holding them accountable for relevant metrics. Smart leaders demonstrate their trust and respect for the expertise they hire, giving them a certain amount of leeway and by default, deferring to their recommendations in subjective areas like design.

Sharing responsibility for timelines

Whenever my team missed a deadline for a client, every case could be traced back to a single cause: the client failed to cooperate in a timely fashion and threw our production team off schedule. It's understandable; things come up for businesses, and they may become too busy to sign off on creative work, to provide written content, or to be available for photography or video projects. But the difference between good leaders and bad ones is how they respond. Leaders with integrity own their mistakes and shortcomings with their agency. They understand changes in time-frames may mean deadlines will change considerably, and the project will cost more. Nothing destroys a good working relationship between a leader and an agency more than when businesses fail to respond, communicate, or provide agreed-upon cooperation in a timely manner. They then demand the agency absorb resulting cost overruns and insist they reschedule other client work to accommodate them when they're eventually ready.

Agreeing up front on expectations

Good agencies are careful to manage a leader's expectations. It's an important exercise for maintaining great relationships between an agency and a client. Good leaders pay careful attention to these conversations and agreements. They understand and agree up front on what to expect, and they don't dream up new expectations on their own. When expected results are reached, they express gratitude to their agency partners.

As I think about the outcome for Charles, I'm saddened knowing this is such a common occurrence. So many small business leaders don't understand how to bring out the best in their agency partners and end up sabotaging any hope of valuable marketing results. Worse, they typically blame the agency for problems and disagreements they caused from their poor leadership.

Effective leaders don't allow committees to take over creative projects. They hire talented creatives and, within certain boundaries, give them space and trust. They understand the bigger picture the agency is working toward and have clear expectations for timelines and results. They take responsibility for their company's involvement, giving timely feedback and cooperation as agreed upon up front.

Having founded and grown a digital agency over the last 12 years, I can affirm nothing brings more joy to my team than doing great work for a well-led company. I know that many other agencies share that attitude. When great leaders bring out the best in great agencies, everyone wins.

CHAPTER SUMMARY

- Overseeing marketing stakeholders can be difficult, and few leaders have the training or experience to do it well.

- Creative work should be performed by a carefully selected individual with talent and experience, not a committee.

- The leader's role is to make sure that the creative work aligns with the business goals, the brand standards, and the intended audience's preferences. Leaders must remember that, in many cases, they're not the audience the creative work is designed to impress.

- Successful leaders respect their marketing stakeholders' production schedules and respond with needed/requested feedback promptly.

- Smart leaders include the necessary people in conversations about marketing projects from the beginning, never bringing new members onto the team mid-way through. They never allow committees to have direct say with marketers, but rather assign a single liaison to filter and to communicate for the collective.

- Leaders must keep in mind that successful marketers develop great user experiences. The creative and design work involved in doing that may not be what they expect or as impressive as they first hoped.

- A website's launch should not be delayed in order to make it perfect. Websites should be perfected over time, once they are live and user behavior can be observed.

How Much Should We Spend?

At a recent presentation to business leaders, I asked them, "If you had an extra $100,000 in your marketing budget, would you know how to effectively spend it? In other words, how would you spend it to see a good return on the investment?"

The room was quiet, and I'm pretty sure I knew what they were thinking. Every business leader I've asked is less confident than they want to be about how to spend marketing dollars. Developing marketing maturity in an organization should be a key role for a leader—to make sure the organization is getting better at spending marketing dollars year-over-year.

As I meet with business leaders, I'm often asked, "How much money should a small business spend on marketing?" I'm aware the government's Small Business Association suggests percentage amounts, adjusting them based on factors like the number of years in business and industry type. I know that in general, a small business might budget seven to eight percent of revenues toward marketing, assuming this investment still leaves profit margins between 10 and

12 percent. But there's one question that isn't considered: how can a company effectively spend marketing dollars?

Spending money effectively on marketing is a learned skill and an ongoing pursuit for any successful organization. In my experience, however, this doesn't occur unless the leadership has a specific vision. But sadly, leaders on many occasions actually prevent a business from developing the necessary marketing systems and measurements year-after-year by their cautious budgeting. That was certainly the case for Mark.

Let's Build Half a Boat

Mark had a very profitable business that repaired leaking basement walls and made them waterproof. Along with his two full-time employees, Mark kept three trucks on the road and their schedules full while serving southern New Jersey.

When Mark came to me wanting help with his marketing, we quickly discovered that a new lead, in his case a phone call or an email generated from his website, would nearly always become a paying client. When prospects called, they were usually ready to hire him on the spot. Leads were like gold to Mark.

Plus, the profit made from one house call was quite significant. With some quick mental math, Mark and my team determined that with just two additional leads per month, the additional profits would pay for the monthly budget we were proposing. Based on our experience in this type of industry and our research, we were confident we could build a lead-generation system that would produce at the pace of 20 to 40 leads a month before the end of the year.

Mark was cautiously interested. Up to this point, he wasn't used to working with an agency. He was getting leads from word-of-mouth and by running radio ads in his service area. But the thought of adding this new marketing expense to his budget gave Mark cold feet. He had the cash flow to support it, but it just seemed like a lot of money.

Mark eventually agreed to "give it a try," but he'd only spend half the amount the strategy required. While we did our best to manage his expectations, months later, Mark was disappointed. Frankly, the money he had spent wasn't bringing any type of return, not even the two leads per month we believed were a safe bet.

The original plan was to build a valuable lead-generation system for Mark. That meant making a lot of important changes on his website so it would convert customers and engaging in a number of activities to drive traffic to it. Even with the most frugal approaches and doing the most minimal work in these areas, the plan was underfunded.

"How far can you sail in half a boat?" I asked Mark one day. "That's what you asked us to do—build half a boat. There's a minimal amount of money that needs to be risked in order to execute any comprehensive strategy. It makes no sense not to make that appropriate investment and then judge the results. You want to build half a boat and see how far it sails, then use that outcome to decide whether or not to budget the appropriate amount. That makes no sense."

Mark may have been better off putting the marketing money in the bank and allowing his business to go on as usual. Budgets need to match strategies, but too often, leaders fantasize they can order a strategy half-executed in order to test it. It's common for leaders to say, "Well let's try spending this much, and if it works out, then we'll spend more." That's terribly foolish, but I've heard it countless times from inexperienced leaders. Leaders can't dip their toes in to test the water of a marketing plan. They need to give it fair consideration with the right budget and enough time, then judge its value.

Sadly, the marketplace is full of agencies with cheap marketing service packages for naive leaders. They target the many leaders out shopping for a marketing approach based on price. But cost must correlate to effectiveness, and only the plans that bring results are truly valuable.

Many small business owners are like Mark. They make budgeting an emotional decision rather than a logical one. They budget based on what they're used to spending rather than on what they need to spend in order to get a great return. They base decisions on feelings instead of proven methods that are a mix of math and guiding principles.

But fear and caution aren't the only emotions I've seen drive bad budget decisions. Too much optimism and ambition can do the same. That was the case for Charlotte.

Fools Rush In

Charlotte was a hard-driving entrepreneur with three successful businesses. Her biggest success, a company that manufactured backyard swing sets, was ripe for growth, and Charlotte was ready to go at it with great energy and optimism.

Charlotte interviewed several marketing agencies and selected one company well-suited to product marketing. She gave them a budget to work with that made the agency's heads spin. Naturally, they smiled so much, their teeth got dry, and Charlotte loved that she was going to be their pet client in the coming year. She could call them any time and make demands, and they were eating out of her hand.

But that year proved to be disappointing. Campaign after campaign was burning through cash and failed to bring in enough sales to justify the expenditure. When the end of the year came, Charlotte's budget was drained, and she gave the agency the news they most dreaded. "I'm sorry, but we're pulling the plug on our marketing with you."

I've seen this happen to many overly optimistic leaders. They are so determined and optimistic about their business, they throw too much money too fast at marketing it. "Go big or go home" is their mantra. They underestimate the amount of time it takes to get traction, develop key insights, and grow all the momentum-generating aspects that make up successful marketing.

Making a full-blown effort at marketing is admirable, but ambitious leaders often find out the hard way they shouldn't spend too much marketing money too quickly. As an agency owner, I've occasionally been put in situations where I've needed more time to experiment and to better understand exactly where and how to make marketing investments that bring positive returns.

Companies need to learn how to spend money, and it can take time to grow into that level of marketing maturity. Sure, any business can buy more and more media exposure with a large budget, but it's likely to be a wasted expense.

It's good to have a starting point for a marketing budget based on industry, margins, goals, and cash flow. Beyond that, however, effective leaders take their organizations on a journey of learning. In three years, will they be ready to spend more money on marketing effectively? It's an ongoing journey, and an organization should constantly be learning. A leader's use of the right budgeting approach is key to that progression. Here are a few common budget milestones that inexperienced marketing leaders mistakenly rely upon.

What are We Used To Spending?

While there are a number of credible ways a business can and should arrive at a marketing budget each year, there's one overarching approach most business leaders use without intention. They budget based on what they spent the year before. Worse, this method is used whether market conditions change, new competitors emerge, strategies are adjusted, or even if results aren't achieved. Leaders get used to spending certain amounts and, by default, use that as their most guiding influence in making budgeting decisions.

My friend Larry is a classic example. He owns a plumbing and heating company. In reviewing his marketing, it was clear he was spending far less than all of his direct competitors. He kept his budget the same even as overall sales were trending downward. Year after year, he was spending an amount he had grown comfortable with.

When he came to my agency to discuss improving his sales numbers through good marketing, he insisted on using the same ineffective budget. I explained to him that regardless of which strategy or which agency he uses, his marketing budget needs to be in line with his competitive environment. Clearly, it wasn't.

What's Left Over?

A common mistake small businesses make, especially start-ups, is neglecting to allocate funds for their marketing budget. The budget is based on what cash might be left over after all other expenses are paid. If there is profit, some of it could be used for marketing.

While it seems absurd to think any competent business person would create a business plan without a reasonable budget for marketing, many do. Smart businesses understand marketing dollars are crucial for business success and therefore have to be planned for in a budget, with the same priority given to utility bills and rent.

A similar mistake is made when businesses experience a downturn. I'm always shocked leaders cut marketing costs during periods when their revenues are down. I've often compared it to cutting down the money tree in the backyard and using it for firewood to save money on fuel bills. It's short-sighted.

Savvy leaders don't determine their marketing dollars based on how much cash is left over. They put them in their budget. They realize they may even need to sacrifice in other areas to have the right amount of cash available for marketing. Wise leaders understand when an organization needs to shift its perspective on marketing expenditures. They also realize that with discipline and time, marketing can become an investment opportunity realized in both near and long-term future profits.

Principles of Budgeting

While budgeting can be made to sound like a left-brained activity, it often has nuances, cash-flow concerns, and even psychological factors like risk-aversion that come into play.

Beyond expenditures that are promotional costs of doing business, marketing investments should bring returns. Frequently, I speak to small business owners who feel safer with a way-too-small marketing budget. However, they often come to realize that if a small budget amount doesn't yield positive results, it's still painful. It's better to spend the "right" amount—one that will yield a positive return. Admittedly, budgeting is not always simple or straightforward. In the past, I've used these four guiding principles:

Prioritize the measurable aspects of your marketing

I've run across small business owners who have spent an entire year's marketing budget on updating their logo and brand standards. This is really unwise for any business for reasons discussed earlier in this book, but also because it leaves no money for the more easily-measured marketing tactics. In the digital age when so many initiatives' success can be tracked, clear attribution models can be developed to correlate and connect advertising spend to actual leads. Businesses cannot neglect branding but must limit their budget on non-measurable marketing activities, making sure that measurable initiatives are used, like direct marketing on digital channels.

Don't drill a hole too low in the ship

This is a gut-check question I often ask myself before I launch into any new financial initiative. If things go south, will we be okay? I'll never take chances that could sink my ship. As leaders budget, they need to consider worst-case scenarios and look at cash flow projections. A marketing budget should not sink a company if takes too long to bring results, or if those results are well below the projected capital returns. While this might seem like common sense, it's not. Entrepreneurs are notorious for risk-taking. Their optimism sometimes drives unrealistic marketing budgets. Even seasoned leaders with entrepreneurial tendencies can make the same mistake. A few years ago, I witnessed countless business leaders dive headlong into the then-new approach we called social media marketing. Agencies sold it; businesses bought it. Everyone agreed a social media presence had value, but few knew how to quantify it or what portion of their marketing budget to allocate toward it. Many dollars were wasted by ambitious leaders overspending on social media strategies because they were enamored with these platforms.

Fail forward fast

Smart leaders pace their spending to optimize their organization's learning. Under-funded marketing will cause strategies to fail or may not fund a campaign adequately enough to gather sufficient data. Successful leaders understand the importance of acquiring marketing savvy through experimentation. They provide sufficient funding while demanding careful analysis of results. That's why leaders may need to spend initial marketing dollars to learn how to spend marketing dollars more effectively in the future—in other words, leaders need to be willing to pay to get marketing experience and insights. Keeping that in mind, leaders need to balance their courage to try new opportunities with ruthless caution, so they don't run out of money as they learn how to spend it.

Find a business case

If you're a business leader wanting to sort out your marketing budget, try starting with this question: "What's the business case for spending money on marketing?" Where is there opportunity within the business? Which of the company's profit-drivers can be amplified through good marketing? What are the marketing problems we need to focus on first? What insights might drive the strategy? Without business objectives, a leader has no milestones for a marketing budget. Thus, there must be a business case.

Sometimes there are multiple profit-driving facets in a company. By segmenting them, a leader can more easily decide how much to spend on each marketing segment. For example, if a company charges $250,000 for a software installation and makes a 50 percent profit margin on that amount, they might be willing to spend from $25,000 to $50,000 to get a new customer. At the same time, if they charge $250 to perform a software update, and their profit margin is only $25, they may only want to spend a few dollars per customer in that area of their business.

Categorizing a Marketing Budget

It happens every year. The CEO of a company calls the team into a meeting to hold them accountable with the power-question, "I spent this amount of money this year. What did I get in return for that investment?"

While I have great respect for any leader who insists on results, asking this question just frustrates stakeholders. The leader doesn't understand that marketing budgets need to be categorized to be fairly evaluated.

For example, if a client comes to us needing her eight-year-old website rebuilt, that marketing expense can't be evaluated in the same category as an online campaign to promote a product. When leaders talk about total numbers for marketing and demand summary results, they're demanding accountability beyond what's possible. That reductionist approach leaders sometimes take is counter-productive and demoralizing to their marketing stakeholders.

Two kinds of marketing expenses

It's helpful to divide marketing expenses into two categories. A business typically needs things like brand development, business signage, business cards, and a website. Each of these use marketing dollars for both their creation and maintenance. These types of expenses are the costs of being in business, and their value is often difficult to measure.

To a certain extent, creating basic brand awareness can be lumped into this category. Sponsoring events, investing in signage, and other tactical efforts to elevate a brand are often necessary to let the world know that a business exists. Every business needs to make some investment of time or money for basic awareness. But leaders often lump cost-of-doing-business expenses into their consideration of that budget's return on investment. That's unrealistic, unwise, and unfair to those asked to give an account.

There's another category of marketing expenses that demands a very different mindset when creating a marketing budget. Expenses related to campaigns, advertising, and certain types of events are good examples. We'll call these "transactional marketing" categories, and they mostly use easily measurable marketing tactics. Leaders have the greatest opportunity for budget refinement in these categories. This is where leaders implement a data-driven approach to determining a marketing budget.

For example, Melissa's landscaping company targeted local audiences with paid advertisements on social media platforms and on major search engines. These advertisements allowed users to click through to landing pages where customers could download a coupon to buy trees at 10 percent off that week. At the same time, Melissa ran a mailing campaign where she put different coupons directly into the hands of local residents. Melissa could directly track the sales that were made from those efforts because they could be connected directly to a sales outcome.

A Data-Driven Approach to Budgeting

When I'm helping business leaders determine a budget for the transactional side of their marketing, we start by gathering information about their business and their sales. It's helpful to involve experienced members of the sales teams in these conversations, as well as someone with a high-level of familiarity with their finances. In those conversations, we need to discover the lifetime value of a customer. Armed with this information, we're able to work backwards and determine what is reasonable to pay to acquire them. This exercise should be the foundation for the transactional side of their marketing budget. Here's a process that works well to determine your customer value:

Determine the profit margin

To start, you should determine the profit margin on one typical unit of sale—or typical service encounter. Most businesses struggle with this calculation. Sometimes it's determined by averages. For example, a grocery store owner may have a wide variety of customer types. Determining the average profit from a customer visit may be best achieved by determining averages from large groups of data in cases like these.

In cases like a pool and spa business, customer types often need to be segmented. For example, those segments would be pool customers and spa buyers each representing very different budgets and profit amounts. This is helpful because profit margins in many businesses can vary greatly from one client sector to the next, and so must budgeting.

Determine the duration of a customer relationship

This is more important for some businesses than others. For example, my own company serves customers on a retainer model, so length of contract is a key element in determining the lifetime value of a client. One-off transactions, like a wedding planner, have one encounter with a customer with no ongoing expectation (hopefully). Business models that expect return business or an ongoing engagement must consider this in calculating the lifetime value of a customer.

Determine the referral rate

What percentage of new customers will make successful referrals to your business? Most businesses are eager to talk about their great word-of-mouth success, but usually as a reason for *not* spending money on marketing. Smart leaders understand the opposite should be true. Businesses that have a high rate of referral from new business can and should justify a much higher budget for marketing because the value of any new client for them is considerably higher. A new client for them represents not only the profit from the transaction, but also the value of transactions from referred business.

What's the lifetime value of a new customer?

The lifetime value of a new customer can be determined using the answers to these questions. Let's use the example of a new lawn and landscape customer. Let's say a typical lawn care client spends $3,000 a year on services. The cost of delivering those services, including labor, adds up to $1,800. That leaves a $1,200 per year profit for lawn care services per client.

But there is more to consider. Those clients usually buy additional products and pay for additional services of varying amounts throughout the year. Taking an average from a large base of customers, that amount is $1,500 per customer annually. The profit margin on those products and services is, on average, $800 after $700 in cost of goods and labor costs are deducted.

The company's net profit from the $3,000 annual service contract, after personnel and expenses are deducted, is $1,200 per year. The additional $1,500 product and service purchases yield $800 in profit for the company. Adding those two amounts totals $2,000 of net profit per customer annually.

Since customers stay with the company for more than three years on average, the lifetime value of the customer is much higher. In this case, $2,000 times three, or $6,000. On top of the three-year-or-longer engagement, the customer successfully refers at least one and often two new customers through their word-of-mouth recommendations during that time frame. Effectively, the lifetime value of a customer using these numbers well exceeds $12,000.

Determine the ratio between leads and conversions

On average, how many leads are needed to generate one customer? Leaders need to make sure the sales and marketing teams are able to have conversations around this important ratio. Most leaders are comfortable giving a good faith estimate on the number of phone calls, email inquiries, or appointments needed to produce one customer. If they aren't, their sales teams are usually able to help them come up with a confident answer. To design and manage marketing budgets effectively, leaders must make sure this information is on the table from the start and that these numbers and ratios are constantly evaluated.

If a sales team gets ten leads from a marketing campaign, it might know from experience that at least 20 percent of those leads will become customers. So five leads would yield one customer, or in other words, the ratio is 5:1.

Many times a business leader is willing to pay ten percent of the value of a new customer. If that lifetime value is, like in our earlier example, more than $12,000, a business leader may be willing to pay ten percent of that value, or $1,200 per customer. If five leads are required to get a new customer, then the business owner would authorize his marketing team to pay, on average, up to $240 per lead.

If this scenario actually existed, the marketing team should be given two directives. The first is to make sure the average cost per lead doesn't exceed $240, which is 20 percent of $1,200. The second is to make sure the quality of the leads remains at that level so the 5:1, or 20 percent conversion ratio remains consistent.

It's Complicated

When faced with this assignment, teams nearly always have the same answer. They say, "Well, we can't determine a value because we have different types of customers." And in nearly every case, they do. But that shouldn't stop them from doing this exercise. They simply need to identify their customer categories and move forward with this exercise for each one of them. For example, a pool and spa company may argue a pool customer is very different from someone who purchases a spa. A pool customer may typically spend $45,000 on an installation, purchase a warranty 75 percent of the time, sign up for a weekly cleaning service 60 percent of the time, buy pool chemicals 50 percent of the time, and refer on average two new customers in the first year. Each of these transactions have different profit margins associated with them, but collectively, a value can be associated with acquiring a new pool customer.

A spa customer may be different. The typical spa customer might spend, on average, $7,300, including the hot tub, cover, upgraded features, delivery, and start-up chemicals. These customers may not sign up for any other services or return after the sale, and they never make referrals. The lifetime value of a spa sale may be very different from the lifetime value of a pool sale. That company's leader should insist on two different marketing budgets because one business sector may justify a budget ten times higher than the other sector.

What percentage of your lead's value are you willing to pay?

The answer to this question will certainly be influenced by many factors, like cash flow, desire for growth, and ability to handle new business. But using this thought process can help leaders better understand the appropriate budget range.

That's especially true for high-value sales. For example, a financial services company may come to realize a new customer has a lifetime value of $40,000 after factoring in profits and likely referrals, and assuming the company converts 25 percent of their leads. That means each lead is worth $10,000. Prior to this consideration, they may have only been willing to pay $25 or less for a lead, when in reality, amounts ten or twenty times that sum could easily be justified.

It's also very helpful for low-margin business leaders who find themselves overspending. I've been asked to conduct national marketing for products with low profit margins. But national marketing is expensive, and unless the leader has some clever publicity or social media stunt in mind to support an organic and viral awareness, there's little hope for a marketing return on investment using expensive direct marketing approaches.

I love digital marketing because it's so measurable. Admittedly, some advertising and promotional areas are harder to measure than others. My advice to businesses interested in building good attribution models is to focus on the measurable marketing channels first.

Many business leaders I've met with over the years are like Mark. Since they don't have a valid way of coming up with a budget, they're guided by their emotions rather than proper analysis. These leaders are paying for "half-a-boat" approaches and getting nowhere year after year, or are overspending before they're ready.

It's the responsibility of the leader to ensure their marketing stakeholders are given the right budgets to work with. With careful attention to the return on investment with specific types of marketing, an organization can improve its ability to spend marketing dollars more effectively year-over-year, even $100,000 more.

CHAPTER SUMMARY

- Smart business leaders are continually learning how to spend marketing dollars more effectively.

- It is critical to budget the right amount for marketing.

- When budgets are too small, strategies can't be properly executed.

- Marketing budgets should not be larger than the company's ability to spend them effectively.

- Leaders shouldn't create marketing budgets based simply on what they're used to spending.

- By segmenting their company's direct marketing budget from other marketing expenditures, leaders can better measure and manage that portion.

- Leaders should build direct marketing budgets based on factors related to the value of new leads.

How Will We Track Progress?

Famous American merchant and religious, civic, and political figure John Wanamaker is often quoted as saying, "Half the money I spend on advertising is wasted; the trouble is I don't know which half."

Evaluating the effectiveness of marketing dollars has always been frustrating. But that was then, and this is now. The digital age has ushered in an unprecedented opportunity for measuring. Years back, when a business produced a brochure, they'd have no way of knowing how many people ever saw it, how long they looked at it, how far down readers' eyes scrolled on each page, or what audiences did after reading it. Today, business owners can study how website visitors arrived on any given page, how long they spent looking at it, what they did next, and in some cases, who the visitor was. Businesses can set up tests that send half the visitors to one version of a webpage, and half to another, commonly called an A/B test. With enough user visits, the better-converting version can be determined and used, moving forward. Design is no longer as subjective as it used to be. New mantras have emerged like, "Always be measuring." Now, a business can go live with two versions, then decide on the best web page layout based on user data rather than the opinions of designers or stakeholders.

Measuring isn't limited to this level of detail. On a macro level, business owners can set up systems where they can track lead sources all the way through to users becoming customers, information that helps inform their advertising investments. Many parts of a business's strategy can be measured, evaluated, and refined.

Most small- to medium-sized businesses I encounter are still not taking advantage of even half of the game-changing digital measurement opportunities available today, approaches that could radically improve their ability to evaluate progress with their digital strategy.

Learn How to Invest

I believe most business leaders are unaware of the opportunities available to them, and they aren't focused on one fundamental aspect of running a company: making sure it's constantly improving in its marketing effectiveness. Still, many more business owners are simply stuck in outdated ways of thinking about and leading marketing.

Prior to the internet, a typical customer would investigate the Yellow Pages, then call a business. In today's information age, consumers' behavior is quite different and typically involves many more "brand touch points" and much more research before a call is made. Today, customers are fiercely independent and generally avoid calling a business until they must. When a customer is asked, "How did you hear about us?" they usually mention one of the many touch points. While it's better than nothing, a leader should have a much higher vision and standard for measuring complex marketing data than relying on a customer's memory.

Successful leaders have an insatiable desire for good marketing data, and that's true even for small businesses. Great businesses can be built on that information.

This was the case for Ned, owner of a plumbing and heating business in my community. When he first started to work with us, he was spending quite a large portion of his revenue on marketing, most of which he wasn't measuring. He went on year after year pouring a lot of his marketing dollars into campaigns he had grown accustomed to running over the years.

Ned had a good website, set to influence and convert visitors. He had a strong brand in the community and a good reputation. He had invested over the years in creating brand awareness in his service area. But Ned was sloppy about how he used his advertising dollars, and he was burning through too much cash each month. He needed to figure out how to drive up his revenues using marketing dollars without getting cash-strapped.

Ned was using a shotgun approach. The tactics that had worked 10 years ago, like direct mail, for example, were getting large portions of his budget, along with online advertisements and radio spots. Worse, Ned wasn't tracking any of these campaigns.

We approached his marketing with a ruthless commitment to making every dollar prove its effectiveness. Some harder-to-measure marketing channels were evaluated by simply ending them and waiting to see if there was any effect. In most cases, there wasn't, and we were quick to reallocate funds. Campaigns that didn't deliver results were either reduced or ended. Channels that were working received more marketing dollars. Over a two-year period, and through a lot of testing and measuring, we were delighted to see Ned's number of leads increase dramatically. Within three years, the size of his business had doubled, his marketing budget was reduced, and his profits were significantly higher, mostly due to cost savings and reallocation of his budget.

The Devil is in the Details

Regardless of how determined a business is to ascertain the return on investment for the entire marketing budget, it can't be done. That's why marketing budgets need to be segmented, as we discussed earlier in this book. Some can be measured with great accuracy using the right systems and tools. Others cannot.

For example, had Ned come to us with a website that didn't perform well, we wouldn't have been able to test awareness campaigns. We would have needed to do some rebuilding of the website so it would have a higher conversion rate. Likewise, if he hadn't already developed his brand awareness, he may have needed to allocate a portion of his marketing budget toward some difficult-to-measure expenditures like local sponsorships and road signage. The effectiveness of those expenditures might have been hard to measure.

Just as not all parts of a marketing budget are easily measured, not all business types lend themselves to simple marketing attribution models like Ned's. For example, a business with a long and complex sales pathway will find measurement especially challenging. It may take a customer years to decide on investing with a financial advisor, or a homeowner may have a relationship with a realtor for 20 years before using their services.

Other businesses are more transactional. For example, local service industries like HVAC, lawn services, local law practices, and roofing companies can usually build powerful marketing attribution models for their businesses. A company can advertise to create awareness, then follow the results using real-time data.

Taking It Further

This was the case for Benjamin. He had a successful gazebo manufacturing and sales business that was positioned to grow into a large national brand. He had worked hard for years to determine where leads were coming from, trying to discern how to drive new orders. But, Benjamin hadn't gone far enough with the measurement demands he was placing on his team. He hadn't connected his marketing metrics to his actual sales metrics.

Benjamin knew how to get leads through marketing. He even knew what types of marketing produced the most leads, where to advertise, and how much he could expect to pay per lead. But he only knew the average value of a lead, not the specific value.

While he knew the cost of a lead, it wasn't until we connected the customer relationship management (CRM) tool his sales team used back to his marketing dashboards that we were able to show Benjamin which lead sources actually resulted in sales. By connecting marketing data to sales data, we could measure which campaigns produced leads that converted and which didn't. This level of marketing attribution detail was transformative.

Using this information to inform our marketing decisions, we could, within months, accelerate Benjamin's sales significantly, creating a several-month backlog in production. What a great problem to have! But not all stories are like Benjamin's, and not all industries are as simple to measure. That was the case for another client we served.

The Middle of the Funnel

Barbara was the founder of a large and growing financial management company for individuals of high net worth. Her business model required a minimum investment of one million dollars in cash. She had a great reputation locally through her community altruism and non-profit sponsorships. Many of her local contacts turned into customers as they accumulated wealth and needed a trusted management firm.

She was in a good position to invest financially in marketing, and given the business she was in, measuring results was a natural behavior. However, creating an attribution model for new business in her industry was more challenging than Barbara was willing to accept. The time between when a customer first learned of Barbara's company and when they engaged with her firm was sometimes 10 years or more.

I remember a meeting when Barbara looked me in the eye and said, "When we surveyed the last 20 new clients and asked them how they heard about us, none of them said 'the internet.'" Clearly it was meant to be an indictment of my agency's work for her company.

I asked her, "How many of those new clients visited your website along the way and were influenced by it? How many of them read online testimonials written by your other clients? How many of them were following your blog posts over the last few years, becoming convinced to use your services?"

She knew most of them had done each of those things, but she was still convinced she had made a valid case against our agency's work because we couldn't clearly demonstrate we had created any customer's initial awareness of her company or captured a lead that became a customer. She was asking the wrong questions because she didn't understand how her own business development strategy worked.

Barbara wanted a marketing attribution model like Benjamin's gazebo business, but that was unrealistic. The sales pathway is very different for one of Barbara's financial advice clients than it is for a gazebo buyer. Businesses that require a great deal of trust, like those selling high-dollar items, and those whose work is not easily reversed, have long and complex sales models. It takes many different brand exposures to build trust. Buyers typically digest a lot of a brand's content along the way, and that part of the customer's journey is also the hardest to measure. Barbara's desire to build a lead generation system that drove clients to her door was not realistic.

As we discussed earlier in our chapter about strategy, the three stages of a sale are initial awareness, then consideration, then decision-making. Since choosing a financial advisor is far from an impulse decision, the consideration phase, the middle section of the sales pathway, is extremely important. Customers might remain in that part of the decision pathway for years—reading blogs, observing social media posts, etc.—before making a decision. Marketing investments need to be made to create the right trust-building experiences over a long period of time. All of these factors make those types of marketing investments the hardest to monetize. The middle layer puts a greater distance between the awareness and the decision steps of the pathway. It adds many multi-faceted and ongoing experiences which make simple attribution models impossible. When a consumer's decision takes years, it's difficult to discern when that first exposure actually happened, or how many additional brand encounters eventually won over the client.

Middle-of-the-sale marketing exercises might include garnering and promoting testimonials, explaining cultural and operational differentiation, providing education, answering common customer questions, addressing specific concerns, disbursing technical information, providing competitive analysis, and promoting in-person events. Typically, this is done by creating valuable and relevant written content (including blogs), webinars, website videos, YouTube channels, podcasts, other social media channels, and well-structured email broadcasts.

How can this be measured best? Leaders who ask, "How many clients are we getting from all this content production?" might find themselves frustrated and may give up on an excellent and effective strategy. Leaders who understand how their marketing investment is supposed to be working are in a better position to evaluate its success.

If I was Barbara, I'd be measuring various parts of my marketing as separate units. I'd measure the beginning of the sales pathway by looking at how much the overall business footprint is growing. I'd track the total 12-month volume of traffic that visits the website. I'd tally that using a 12-month rolling indicator of website traffic. While these could border on being vanity metrics, I'd keep track of numbers like subscribers, followers of the various channels used, and social media mentions, to see how many people are actively aware of the business's existence and to make sure that number is increasing year-over-year. I'd observe this data to determine whether or not my brand's awareness was growing.

For the middle of the sales funnel, the interest or consideration phase, I'd be paying attention to other performance indicators. I'd be tracking how long a typical website visit lasted. I'd note which articles were getting traction, the click-through rate on videos, the percentage that watched the entire video, which pages customers visited after watching a video, and the open rate and click-through rate from emails that were being sent. I'd be tracking how the number of subscribers was growing on my company's content channels, like my blog, podcast, or video channel.

For measuring the last stage of the sales pathway, conversion, I'd look for clues as to what life events correlate to decision making. I'd study which types of in-person experiences produce positive decisions, and how they can be replicated.

While these suggestions border on being too simplistic and

case-specific, the take-away for every leader is the need to understand how sales pathways work and which measurements make the most sense. Ideally, every leader should want a closed loop from "how the customer first heard about the business" to "sales," but this isn't always possible. When it isn't, leaders should insist on measuring portions of the customer's sales pathway separately.

Beware of Vanity Metrics

While this is good advice for Barbara, caution should be taken. When businesses measure only portions of a sales pathway, they run the risk of getting off track. That was the case for my friend Bonnie.

Bonnie had a company that provided customer software development. To an extent, her company could advertise, capture leads, and convert them to sales. But that sales scenario was the exception, not the rule, due to the complex nature of Bonnie's products, the number of decision-makers typically involved, and the difficulty of the software integration. Because of this, Bonnie decided to focus on working on the middle of the sales pathway, like Barbara. She was going to position herself as an expert in her field by creating content and disbursing it through social media channels.

But Bonnie got off track. She started to measure things that, in the end, didn't matter. How many followers did she have on Twitter? How many people liked her company's Facebook page? How many people watched the funny cat video she included in her YouTube Channel? How many people were coming to her website who weren't really candidates to become customers because of their locations? She used software to acquire LinkedIn connections and Twitter followers. By Bonnie's key performance indicators, she was seeing success.

After three years, Bonnie was no closer to growing her business than when she started. The followers she had garnered were not potential customer candidates and never would be. Bonnie, blinded by meaningless data, couldn't see her own lack of progress.

Leaders can become distracted by vanity metrics. These are achievements that may seem impressive but may not make a real contribution to the strategy's overall success. Leaders must pay attention to which numbers matter and which don't over time.

Realistic Timelines

Dan was a hard-driving entrepreneur who hired my firm to launch his start-up business that sold, on average, $200 items online and distributed them through an established retailer network. We took great care to organize a strategy and outline a plan, explaining it to him over the course of several meetings.

Since we were essentially starting from scratch, it was going to be a big job launching this new initiative. But based on our experience with other companies similar to his, we were confident we'd get traction in one to two years. Dan was on board to give it a try. At least that's what we thought.

On month six, a very hard-to-console Dan showed up at our office angry and ready to fire us. He was wondering what we had done and why his business wasn't taking off yet. He was running short on cash much faster than he had planned, and in his eyes, it was our fault. Our marketing plan hadn't delivered, or so he believed.

Like many leaders, Dan didn't consider or budget for the expected timeline for success. Many times, marketing plans don't bring a great return on investment initially, especially for new businesses. It can take time to build out the fundamental marketing assets, like the brand's design elements, a good website, and in his case, product packaging. Dan wanted to go from zero to 100 instantly. His naive expectation was "dollar in, dollar out" from the first month. Comprehensive strategies don't work that way.

Every type of marketing has an expected scenario for when it will bring a return. For example, running an online advertisement campaign might bring a quick return and drive immediate sales for a roofing company. But a content strategy for an environmental consulting company that aims to position their founder as a subject matter expert, creating celebrity status around that leader, may require a five-year timeline.

Adding to that reality, a graph of marketing success is rarely a straight line from start to finish. More typically, it looks like a hockey stick. For example, a quite-famous content marketing expert once revealed to my business group his success trajectory, a graph showing the number of his followers year-over-year. For several years, his growth was painfully slow. Most would have given up. But several years in, his content began getting attention. Soon his subscriber count soared. The graph looked like a hockey stick. This is quite common for businesses that use a content strategy. Sometimes businesses have to work for years at their marketing in order to enjoy what everyone else calls "overnight success."

Crucial Perspectives

Some plans ramp up quickly. Others take longer. If a leader doesn't have a realistic expectation for the timeline and the success trajectory of the marketing strategy, they won't be in a position to make a fair assessment along the way, have the required emotional fortitude, or do advanced cash management planning.

Without the big-picture understanding of how the selected strategy should work, a leader may pull the plug on a campaign prematurely or fail to budget cash flow sufficiently to accommodate a longer-term return on investment.

Leaders must also keep in mind that at the end of the day, marketing is a series of ongoing experiments. Experienced marketers can provide leaders with some predictive models, but unless a leader has a frame of reference for how it's supposed to work and just the right amount of tolerance for error, they won't be in a position to make wise judgment calls. Deciding whether to press forward or pull the plug on marketing initiatives is nearly impossible without a realistic frame of reference.

As leaders grow in their marketing savvy, they more clearly understand the bigger picture of their marketing plans and how they can and should be measured. In my experience, most leaders are big-picture thinkers, and with a bit of effort, they're able to wrap their heads around a marketing strategy, at least from a high level. With that perspective, they're much more likely to guide their organizations to great success.

Leaders who capture a vision for marketing and attribution systems are a great asset to the organizations they serve. However, most leaders who capture a vision for successful marketing are far too optimistic about what can be achieved in a year. At the same time, they underestimate where they could be in three years with the right plan, budget, and unwavering commitment. These same leaders fail to reach these longer-term heights because they grow soft in their resolve halfway through. Effective leaders have both vision and grit. Smart leaders ask, "How will we measure success?" They look for every opportunity to measure all of their marketing dollars but understand that certain parts deserve greater scrutiny. They try to connect awareness campaigns to sales whenever possible but understand certain sales models are complex and benefit from measuring separate parts of the sales journey.

Smart leaders look at the right metrics for their individual strategy and weigh its overall success against a realistic timeline. While yesterday's leaders like John Wanamaker lowered their standards for measuring and pressed forward in faith, today's best leaders have an unwavering devotion to effective measuring, a position that provides an enormous business advantage.

CHAPTER SUMMARY

- Business leaders have a responsibility to ensure tracking systems are in place to measure marketing results—findings that will inform future marketing and budget decisions.

- Budgets need to be segmented to be properly evaluated.

- Leaders should insist on reports that connect marketing data with sales data.

- Complex sales, ones that take a longer time to close, are hardest to measure and should be segmented by the three marketing objectives: awareness, consideration, and decision.

- Leaders should be careful not to use vanity metrics to measure progress.

- Leaders should have a clear, up-front understanding of the expected timeline for any strategy's success, then give that strategy's execution the appropriate amount of time to come to fruition before pivoting.

- Leaders should be constantly experimenting with tactics and learning from those experiments.

What Are We Learning?

Several years back, I was asked to help a manufacturer and national retailer take a high-priced product to market. His then five-million-dollar small business was built on a single source of leads: paid search on Google. Through his use of that platform, he had discovered several specific highly-populated locations in the United States that were ripe for buying exactly what he was producing. When I was finished with my engagement with him, he made sure to remind me of the non-disclosure agreement we had.

At the time, I thought he was being over-protective and excessively concerned. After all, surely his insight about those receptive markets was widely known. Or was it?

Two years later, when I was hired by his direct competitor, I came to learn he was right. He'd had a very valuable marketing insight at the time, and it was key to his success in those years. As a matter of integrity, I never shared that knowledge with his competition, and it soon became obsolete. But it taught me a lesson. Marketing insights are extremely valuable, and the business that obtains and leverages them wins.

One of the goals of successful marketing is to constantly pursue key insights. Smart leaders view marketing insights as valuable and proprietary information that can be a lynchpin for creating competitive advantage. They make sure all of the marketing stakeholders are continually acquiring and refining those insights and using them to their fullest advantage. That's why smart leaders constantly challenge their marketing stakeholders with the question, "What are we learning?"

From Talking to Listening

In our last chapter, we talked about the importance of measuring and tracking the success and progress of a business's marketing strategy. This chapter takes it a step further. Smart business leaders make sure their organizations are not only keeping score on progress, but intentionally learning how to do it better. That said, I'm quite sure that if I surveyed a group of business leaders asking them to make of list of tasks in leading marketing efforts, no one would mention learning. Most leaders don't think of marketing this way. That's understandable. Only a few decades ago, listening or learning was less a part of marketing than it is today. That's especially true for smaller businesses. Yes, we had the occasional focus group study and market research firms, but marketing was mostly about broadcasting messages and creating impressions.

With the information age, consumers can now use the internet to have an *interactive* experience. They can choose what they'd like to see and hear about a brand with a click of the mouse. They can determine which page to look at next with a tap of their thumb on their smartphone. They can express their opinions about brands and learn what others are saying. They can now call, chat, email, book, reserve, and map a business right from their device.

Consumers are now acting and reacting in real time, and this has created an unprecedented opportunity to measure marketing effectiveness, to learn from it, and to evolve and improve quickly. Marketing used to involve mostly one-way communication. Rapidly, it shifted to involve measurable interactive opportunities, consumer activities that can be measured, tested, and developed for better consumer response rates. So why then would so few leaders talk about marketing in terms of learning?

There are two kinds of leaders today. Those who by default still think marketing is about creating messages, advertising, and getting more leads, and those who by choice persistently ask their marketing stakeholders, "What are we learning?" In my experience, many leaders are still stuck in old, long-standing ways of thinking about marketing. They aren't driving their stakeholders to aggressively gain insights and grow from them.

Failing Forward

While professional marketers are notoriously confident about their recommendations, history proves marketing is always experimental. No one really knows how well a new website will perform when it's launched or how a new billboard will influence people when it's posted. The difference is that today, we can easily and efficiently apply scientific methods and statistical analyses to our marketing experiments. Any marketing campaign can and should be thought of as a hypothesis; for example, "If we show this on a webpage, we believe the user will do that." In a relatively short period of time, we can see whether we're correct and change the webpage if necessary, then test our next hypothesis.

Yesterday's marketers confidently ran campaigns and were rarely held accountable, especially by small businesses who couldn't justify the expense of market research. Today's marketers think of a marketing action as a hypothesis to test. Here's what that looks like.

Testing, 1, 2, 3...

Tom had a successful roofing company just outside a mid-sized city. He was interested in seeing it grow, and based on his research, he had an opportunity to gain a significant amount of market share in the next two years. One of his competitors had moved out of the area. Tom would be competing to capture that portion of the local service area against two other similarly-sized roofing companies. Tom understood the next two years would be important for him to make an aggressive grab at the market through effective advertising.

Tom investigated various online advertising opportunities on search engines and social media platforms and narrowed it down to a few he believed best aligned with his marketing strategy and his audience. With each of his campaigns, however, his website was going to be the hub. All of his marketing was counting on his website to convince and convert visitors.

Tom was fortunate. He had engaged with an agency that encouraged him to constantly test his campaigns and to adapt quickly. For example, his company created two versions of a key landing page to see which one had the best conversion rate. Tom's business was localized, and he didn't have the high volume of traffic typically needed for statistically relevant results when doing a test like this. But he knew that if one page strongly out-performed the other, he'd gain an important insight, even with only a few thousand visitors. And that's exactly what happened.

Tom's first landing page suggested visitors call now for a free quote, a call-to-action all Tom's competitors were using. But Tom's second version of the landing page encouraged visitors to use a do-it-yourself estimator Tom had developed. It was a big hit, and visitors were not only using it, they were sharing it with friends.

That early discovery of what visitors really wanted launched his company far ahead of his competition and enabled him to capture the market share he was after. All of this occurred because Tom viewed marketing as an experiment.

Experiments like Tom's can be used for any type of marketing campaign where landing pages are involved, but other broader insights can be gained about a website in general. For example, websites that have been live for any length of time have performance histories. These data show how visitors are finding the website and navigating through it. While successful leaders don't need to be able to open up analytics programs and diagnose a website's user pathways, they should be concerned if their marketing stakeholders are not experimenting. Leaders should insist that the marketing team has a culture of learning.

That was the case for a private college I consulted with several years back. The leadership team sat around a board table while I showed them how a large portion of their enrollment traffic was using the website, arriving at a "dead-end" user experience, then leaving the website. The Director of Admissions wouldn't let me leave the meeting without a promise that my company would bring a proposal to fix their website immediately.

If a business hosts an event, good leaders make sure there's a good event coordinator in place so everyone has a good experience. Imagine an event where people arrive and then find it difficult to get where they need to in the building, or they're sent from place to place to find the refreshments. Imagine an event where more than half the people arrive at the front door, then turn around and leave out of disappointment or confusion. Any responsible business pays attention to whether or not people are being served and whether they're having a positive experience at an event.

Then why don't more leaders insist the same care is given to the website's visitors? Countless websites have visitors clicking link after link trying to find information, creating frustration, and driving them away. It's inexcusable.

Even good websites can constantly evolve and improve. Smart leaders make sure the user's experience is prioritized in every website conversation, and that it's constantly evaluated and improved.

That was the case for Sarah's weight loss business. Her company had a unique approach for helping postmenopausal women control their weight through hormone therapy. Since most of her visitors weren't familiar with her approach, she used her website to provide a lot of information and post compelling user testimonials. Because Sarah had a team of astute marketers helping her, and because Sarah asked them the right questions, she discovered a game-changing insight.

Visitors who viewed her video explaining how hormones affect weight were 3.5 times more likely to contact Sarah's company before leaving the website than those who hadn't viewed the video. Sarah's team had initially believed testimonials were going to be the primary influence. They posted them throughout the site and encouraged users to "See what others are saying." They even had a video of people talking about how the program helped them.

But the user data showed otherwise. The video that explained the science behind body changes was discovered to be the silver bullet. Using that insight, the site was changed, and many of the information pages had a new call to action: "Watch this brief video to learn how hormones affect weight." The website's overall conversion rate increased significantly, improving campaign results and return on investment across numerous traffic-driving advertising. All of this happened because Sarah's team was determined to learn more about how their marketing was working, and they took a careful look at the website users' behaviors.

A Finished Publication or a Work In Progress?

After serving as CEO for four years at a local fencing company, Rachel was approached to rebuild her website. "We can build you something much more evocative that what you currently have," argued Michelle, owner of a branding and website design firm across town. Michelle and Rachel had met for lunch to discuss how, in Michelle's words, she was helping other companies like Rachel's.

"We've got arguably the best creatives and designers in the region. No other firm has won even half of the awards our team has," Michelle bragged. "Already this year, we've launched five websites, and the clients are over-the-top pleased."

Michelle was used to selling her services to leaders by appealing to their sense of vanity and desire to create an impressive brand. Indeed, her team could make beautiful websites with jaw-dropping designs. But frankly, Michelle and her team had no idea if they were increasing or decreasing conversion rates on the websites they built. She assumed—and allowed her customers to share her assumption—that a better-looking website was better for a business.

Rachel was smart and didn't buy into the vision Michelle was selling. While she knew her website needed to be refreshed and that some of its design aspects were a bit dated, she wasn't going to throw away years of learning. There was no way Rachel would ever allow a company like Michelle's to completely tear down her company's existing website and replace it.

Since the beginning of her tenure as CEO, Rachel had been making sure team members were measuring and incrementally improving their website's performance one test at a time. They had invested years into understanding exactly what type of navigational experience worked best. They understood which were the most successful layouts for important pages, which calls to action to use, and how to best present them. Rachel was willing to refresh the general look and feel of the design, but other than that, the user experience her team had eventually created was working brilliantly. Compared to other fencing company websites, it was out-performing industry milestones by five times, even with a slightly dated design.

Smart leaders like Rachel understand websites aren't creative works, they're ongoing opportunities for optimization, an exercise that will pay off immensely over time.

Unfortunately, many business leaders still think of their websites as static publications or online brochures. They approach interactive media the same way they've always approached creative work. Companies like Michelle's prey on these leaders, giving them what they want—award-winning design with no mention of learning or incremental change after launch, let alone accountability for the site's performance. Businesses like Rachel's aren't built on award-winning website design; they depend on their users having effective website experiences. And successful websites like Rachel's are built over time and through user testing.

Rachel's team had stumbled upon some game-changing business insights as they worked with the website. Some of them had to do with how they worded things, some pertained to the order in which images or videos were presented, and some were based on how things were placed on pages. It was a collection of micro- and macro-discoveries that collectively had turned their website into a high-performing conversion machine.

But Rachel's team had done more than website conversion optimization for their successful fencing company. Along the way, they had created website content that had earned links from a variety of local organizations and websites, sources of traffic and leads.

They had experimented with a variety of advertising channels and had narrowed down which ones performed best and which campaigns drove the most high-conversion traffic. They learned which areas in their 50-mile service radius were most receptive to marketing, which weeks of the year worked best for advertising, and even how weather correlated to customers responding to campaigns.

Through careful study of their audiences' reactions to marketing campaigns, Rachel's team had discovered some core insights about their customers. Specifically, they learned some of their customers were mostly concerned with the quality and long life of the fence, others were focusing more on privacy, and a third group cared mostly about the beauty as people drove by their property.

Learning how to talk about their products and services in a way that best resonated with each of these three audience groups was as important as any of their discoveries. Prior to this, Rachel's company had gotten used to using language created by manufacturers and making assumptions about why people chose to install fencing.

Marketing from the Factory Floor

My friend Steve had a similar learning experience to Rachel's. He founded and ran a solar company that served three markets: residential, agricultural, and industrial. Each of these segments represented very different types of buyers, so it made sense to provide very different experiences for each. Steve's team created three main links with images on the homepage and labeled them, "residential, agricultural, and industrial."

When we started looking at how the website (which we didn't build) was performing, we were disappointed about the high bounce rate, the number of people who arrived at the site and then left right away before clicking on other pages. This deserved more research.

We did five-second impression tests with hundreds of volunteers asking them the question, "If you were shopping for solar solutions for your house, where would you click on this page?" To our astonishment, almost no one said they would click on "residential." Why? Because homeowners didn't relate to that word. That was what Steve's company called their audience, but it wasn't a word the audience naturally related to themselves. Steve's team was making a very common business marketing mistake; they were marketing with their language, not their customers' language. They were marketing from the factory floor.

In many cases, businesses inadvertently use language they've become used to but their customers haven't. My own industry, digital marketing, is notorious for doing just that. I've needed to stop myself many times from using acronyms like SEO and PPC in client meetings, terms which sometimes confuse and frustrate some of the less "techie" leaders, the very people I'm trying to help.

Before You Cross the Desert

Learning as part of marketing also plays out for product research. This was certainly true for my friend, and consummate entrepreneur, Stuart. He owned several businesses, including one that built and shipped ready-to-assemble outdoor pavilions.

Stuart and I had lunch during a time when he was considering whether or not to begin carrying electrical packages for his outdoor structures, like ceiling fans and lighting. When he asked for my opinion, I'm sure my answer surprised him. I suggested he started marketing to find out.

Naturally, he first objected. He couldn't advertise something if he didn't have it for sale. Or could he?

My team helped Stuart put together some advertisements for his new (potential) product. As customers responded and tried to make a purchase, they were informed that the product was not currently available before the transaction was completed. From this exercise, Stuart not only discovered whether there was market interest in his products, but he was also able to experiment with different price-points to gauge what would be optimal.

Like most leaders, up to that point, Stuart thought of marketing as influencing. Now he understands that well-measured marketing becomes a valuable research tool.

As I explained to Stuart, his idea was like an oasis located far away in the desert. He knew that if he survived the journey, he'd be in a wonderful place. But many business initiatives die on their way to paradise. That's why leaders should do market research before taking big risks. Not only do many business owners push new ideas forward using optimism instead of research, they also believe marketing should be able to take their potentially bad idea and make it a success. They're mistaken. You can't market your way out of a bad business idea.

Marketing research is not only useful in deciding whether or not to launch a new product or service, it can also provide key tactical guidance. For example, savvy content producers are constantly paying attention to trending topics to inform their subject matter.

Have a lawn and landscape company? Why not stay up with the latest tree disease or invasive species homeowners in your area are researching? Trying to decide what blog post would be read, video watched, or podcast listened to? Check out what people are searching for on Google using some of Google's free tools, or start searching for similar content and see how much attention it's receiving.

Leadership Perspectives

Smart leaders no longer view marketing as a way to simply

create brand awareness or promote sales. In the information age, they recognize it as a tool for research, listening, and vital guidance.

Some leaders are naturally analytical and curious. Using marketing as an opportunity for learning comes naturally to them. Other leaders simply need to regularly ask the question, "What are we learning?" to keep analytical and curious stakeholders focused and evolving.

Smart leaders view marketing knowledge as extremely valuable property developed over time. They understand it's an ongoing pursuit because it's constantly changing. It doesn't happen by accident. It takes deliberate effort, skill, and organizational discipline. The best leaders have a vision for this happening in their organizations, and they make sure the right people are in place with the right budgets and necessary support.

They not only pay attention to what their organizations are learning, but they also note their pace of development. It reminds me of the joke about how fast you need to run from an attacking bear—just a little faster than the friend behind you. The same is true for gaining competitive insights. Depending on the competitive nature of an industry, businesses may need to devote more time and attention in staying one step ahead of competitive marketing forces.

Marketing involves research, experimentation, and listening. Of course, that will only happen with the right stakeholders, the right measuring, and continual testing and learning. The greater insights often require an intuitive look at the larger landscape of trends and patterns. Many leaders are good at picking up on these game-changing insights. Whether or not that's the case, certainly every leader should be able to ask his marketing stakeholders, "What have we learned about marketing in the last year?" and get a satisfactory answer!

CHAPTER SUMMARY

- Marketing insights are valuable to business.

- Smart leaders view marketing metrics as opportunities to learn, grow, and improve on future marketing efforts.

- Leaders should accept that best practices in marketing involve ongoing experimentation and iterative improvement.

- Smart marketers are always testing campaigns, observing any correlations between user behavior and conversions, and looking for patterns of success.

- Smart businesses use the language of their potential customers in their marketing.

- Leaders can use digital marketing to test the marketing receptiveness of potential products or services.

- Smart leaders view marketing knowledge as extremely valuable property developed over time.

Where Do We Start?

Jim's Story

Jim came into my office to talk about growing market share for his law practice. He knew the firm's website was very out-of-date, and they hadn't focused on their marketing for several years.

After a bit of small talk, Jim got down to business. "If we hired your team, what would you do for us?" he asked.

This came as no surprise to me. It's a common way leaders kick off these initial marketing conversations with agencies like mine. They want to see a plan so they can evaluate how they feel about it, whether or not they're comfortable with the price, and whether or not they believe my team can execute it. As we've discussed earlier in this book, this is a dangerous pathway inexperienced leaders take in making marketing decisions. They feel like if they hear the right plan, they'll just know it.

Leaders often have an amazing ability to make decisions using gut instincts. But when a business has neglected their marketing for years, they may need a different type of leadership skill: *prioritization.*

As is often the case, Jim's marketing was in shambles. Not only were new prospects deciding not to use his firm after viewing his website, many more weren't even finding it. Google wasn't listing his web pages very high on the search results pages, and worse, was sending potential clients to his direct competitors' websites. When visitors did find his business online, they became frustrated. Most were using mobile devices, but his website wasn't designed for small screens or for a mobile user's thumb. Navigation was difficult, and much of the text was too small to read without panning and scanning.

Jim's website looked about the same as when he'd had it built several years earlier. He hadn't added new content or paid any attention to how users typically navigated through it. Building a new website wasn't going to make up for years of neglect in creating relevant content.

His firm had an assortment of reviews posted on a few different websites, but many of them were negative. Jim's team hadn't asked for direct feedback from clients, so over the years, their occasional unhappy clients took their complaints to the internet. His firm had neglected to implement any type of system for monitoring this, or for garnering positive reviews from the great majority of their clients who loved the firm. Overall, Jim's neglect of their internet review landscape had allowed an unfair and inaccurately poor reputation to grow online, a factor that was having a significant negative effect on prospects' decisions. Worse, Jim and his team had no idea this was happening.

These weren't Jim's only problems. Two years earlier, his firm had bought out another smaller practice and moved their office. Later, they added another partner to their practice's name. Subsequently, online directories were mostly inaccurate. There were five different versions of the business name, collected over the 15 years since they'd opened. There were six different phone numbers mixed into the web's information ecosystem. They had three different addresses, including one partner's personal residence. Web surfers searching for them by name found grossly incorrect information. Potential clients were shown the wrong address on Google maps, and many new or potential clients were finding incorrect contact information and becoming frustrated.

Google's algorithm noticed the inconsistencies to their name, address, and phone number mentions on the web, and consequently didn't list them in local search results, even when nearby prospects were searching for the specific services the firm offered. Their Google business page wasn't updated, which highlighted their negative review profile, listed the wrong URL for their website, and didn't have their hours of operation.

Even though Jim's firm specialized in labor law, none of their branding aligned with their specialty. Everything about their brand suggested they were a big corporate firm when the opposite was true. They were a boutique firm that helped individuals with labor claims.

Jim's firm had run a few advertisements over the years that had created local awareness. They'd bought some billboard space using the typical photo of their partners wearing dark suits, arms crossed, standing resolute, and not smiling. The tagline said, "We get the job done." This lack of brand clarity had done more to confuse their local audience than to build business momentum.

They had no real system to evaluate their marketing budget's effectiveness. When they did receive the occasional call from a prospect, they had no way to track where the lead had come from. The secretary was trained to ask, "How did you hear about us?" but no one ever said, "I saw your billboard."

Like many business leaders, Jim came to me seeking an instant results-producing marketing campaign. He wanted to find out if we had any tricks up our sleeves. But Jim was looking for the wrong thing.

To use a metaphor, Jim was interested in looking at plans for a new kitchen when his house's foundation was cracked, his roof was leaking, there was a sinkhole in his driveway, and termites were eating the supporting beams. Leaders like Jim shouldn't be asking, "What's the one thing that really works?" but rather, "Where do we start?"

Businesses that have not engaged in effective and relevant marketing efforts for a few years, like an old house, tend to accumulate a lot of deferred maintenance. Many times, business leaders are unaware just how badly their marketing efforts have fallen behind or the length of time and financial investment likely required to realize the benefits of marketing momentum. They're unaware that any number of crucial foundational pieces are broken, and because of it, there's rarely a single strategy that will rescue them.

That's why we typically see the best results and returns on marketing investments in the second and third years of engagements with businesses, especially those like Jim's. And that's why businesses that demand impressive results in the first year may be setting unrealistic expectations for themselves and their marketing stakeholders.

Inexperienced leaders view marketing as advertising to get new business. Smart leaders understand marketing is more like turning a large, heavy flywheel. You keep adding push after push to gain momentum. Like the old house with deferred maintenance, businesses like Jim's may even have a negative marketing momentum which must be turned around with their audience's perceptions, with Google's algorithm, and with the large and complex online information ecosystem.

With that realistic and powerful analogy, wise leaders also understand the amount of time required to truly get momentum and the need to have some business-generating "wins" along the way. For many business leaders, the question shouldn't be about strategy, it should be about priority. What can we work on this year that will bring the best benefit in the short term but also contribute to the two- or three-year vision?

If Jim had asked me where to start, I would have suggested prioritizing the timeless basics of marketing his firm's brand. He first needed to understand clearly how he wanted his firm to appear. This exercise would also include the decision about who he was trying to reach, the consistent image his firm needed to present, and the appropriate language and wording that supported this overarching brand position. Since Jim hadn't done this marketing exercise effectively in the past, their billboard campaigns didn't create effective awareness or resonate with the firm's intended market. In fact, they had confused his audience, a problem that needed to be undone. Creating a brand position needs to come first, and when done effectively, it will amplify all other marketing efforts.

That's exactly what happened for my friend, Dan. Dan owned a CPA firm that offered unique, online, CFO-type financial management services for small businesses. He was trying a little of this and a little of that but wasn't able to generate leads.

My team suggested that rather than looking like every other CPA firm out there, he should consider positioning himself as an expert at serving one type or a few types of business(es). He chose to specialize in working with marketing agencies, and within two months, he had generated some helpful and unique content for the agency world. He made small adjustments to his website to align with this new brand position and posted his new content there.

While it was unusual to see such immediate results, we were

thrilled that within a few months, Dan had not only picked up a few new agencies as clients, he had gotten the attention of the country's largest organization for small agencies in the United States. He received an invitation to participate in educational events, which would most likely prove to be a high-performing lead-generation activity, better than any amount of advertising spend he could've afforded.

Dan's success tracks back to him focusing on the right priority—his brand's position. With that decision made, he could align his other marketing activities around his brand. In Dan's case, that meant changing the overarching description of his business and the content he created to show he was truly focused on serving agencies.

At least half the time a business approaches our firm, they come for one service but in fact need many. If they're not aware of how much work needs to be done, their budget will be inadequate and their time-frame unrealistic. Inexperienced leaders shop for a marketing silver bullet, but savvy leaders understand a brand position is a silver thread that is woven through multiple marketing activities.

What's the Business Case?

Some businesses do have a clear brand position and are looking for a strategy. That was the case for Cheryl, the CEO of a successful dermatology and aesthetic medicine center. With three locations, nine doctors and 30 employees, they'd gained traction as a business but were uncertain how to get to the next level.

When I sat down with Cheryl, she was eager to talk about the approach we should take. From the beginning of our conversation, I was impressed with Cheryl's knowledge and vocabulary about marketing. She talked about SEO, even domain authority, as though they were household terms. She wanted to know what we thought about a more robust content strategy, a specific plan using social media, and how we might use paid search. Obviously, Cheryl had done some reading and was ready to engage in a marketing conversation.

I think I surprised Cheryl when I dodged her questions and turned the conversation back to her business. I asked her, "What's the business case for your marketing spend this year and the years to come? Where do you see opportunity for growth? Which, if any, parts of your service offerings or audience sectors do you see diminishing?"

This shift in the conversation seemed disorienting for Cheryl. It was clear to me she hadn't thought about it recently. She wasn't necessarily looking for a marketing strategy directly connected to a business objective. It's a common mistake.

In Cheryl's case, we were eventually able to determine her real opportunity would be ramping up her service to her male clientele, businessmen who were becoming increasingly open to improving their appearance. Cheryl realized that because of her office locations near businesses where there were many male professionals, her higher number of male employees, and the business networks in which she was involved, she would be able to grow and maintain this lucrative, relatively untapped market much more easily than her competitors could. With that insight and business plan, we were able to craft the right approach and create the right content to reach and persuade this audience.

Using the knowledge about what their existing male customers had asked for and the reasons they made appointments, Cheryl and her team understood what their growing male clientele wanted. With more of a focus on fitness, her male clients were spending time at the gym and at the pool. Many of them were self-conscious about excessive body hair and were looking for discreet solutions. Cheryl began promoting hair removal services for men by running local ads. She leaned into the obvious awkwardness of the topic by making a big hairy bear her brand's mascot and made her advertising tagline, "Don't be the bear."

Cheryl asked her marketing agency to tweak the brand colors to make them less feminine and more gender-neutral. She even changed her waiting rooms to look and feel less like a medi-spa, transforming it into a minimalistic and modern professional environment that she believed would appeal to both sexes.

Adding to that, Cheryl's team launched a blog targeted at men who desire a professional look. Her team published information about men's skin care, popular hair treatment, shaving tips, and common aesthetic medical procedures that can make a big difference for men who want to look their best.

Had Cheryl engaged in general marketing and lead-generation campaigns for each of her business's services, she would certainly have spread out her limited marketing budget across all of her marketing segments rather than concentrating it on her best opportunity. Two years later, her business had added 30 percent to her top line, far out-pacing her competition. Concentrating her marketing efforts on her best opportunity paid off.

Start at the Bottom of the Funnel

When business leaders approach me to talk about marketing and ask where they should start, my answer is usually the opposite of what they expect. They think I'm going to tell them about top-of-marketing-funnel opportunities, like a cool new place to advertise. Instead, I audit the bottom of their funnel. Do they have an online experience ready that will convert prospects and stay in touch with them? Most don't.

Take the example of Harry, a local chiropractor who got an average of 4,000 unique visits a month to his website. He wanted to grow his business and asked me how he could do some online marketing to get more clients. Looking at his website's user data, only half of one percent ever filled in a contact form, clicked to call, or downloaded a new patient form. These important conversions weren't happening, and visitors left without taking any meaningful or measurable action.

I explained to him that to move from 4,000 visitors to 8,000 visitors in his relatively small market would be difficult and require a considerable commitment of time and money. But to change his conversion rate from one half of one percent up to two percent was entirely possible, could happen relatively quickly, and would add value equal to having 16,000 visitors. Conversion rate is the multiplier that takes "awareness" and makes it valuable.

The great majority of businesses I work with have the best opportunities for early momentum by looking at the bottom of their marketing funnel, not the top. Their first exercise should be conversion optimization across all of their prospects' experiences. For some businesses, that means looking at the readiness of their sales team. For most businesses, it means creating an optimized website user experience, and an improved online presence, including review profiles, that convert visitors into contacts, connections, or customers.

Measure and Learn from the Start

Experienced leaders understand that advertising not only brings value by driving sales and business leads, it also brings data used to refine future marketing budgets. But this only happens when an organization understands how important it is to be measuring.

Most inexperienced business leaders I've worked with over the years begin marketing without a bigger plan for gathering data. While I suspect this will change in the next decade, at the time of writing this, I rarely encountered a small business with a good system for connecting data about advertising to completed sales. In other words, their marketing data isn't connected to their customer relationship management system. This is especially true with those having high value, complex sales, and longer sales cycles.

Great leaders ask, "Where do we start?" and understand that the right answer involves readiness for measuring their marketing effectiveness.

Set Priorities

Certainly, there's no one-size-fits-all approach to setting priorities in marketing or choosing where to start. Even when certain marketing concerns are prioritized, the amount of resources used to address any one of those concerns often needs to be throttled back in order to address others.

For example, a few years back, we helped a dental practice grow their marketing share in the surrounding community. They needed to work on their positioning and branding. We chose to limit the budget on branding concerns so we'd have funds for conversion optimization.

Meanwhile, the dentist's direct competition went all-out in branding efforts, spending disproportionate amounts on photo shoots and advertising in local lifestyle magazines. While both dental practices prioritized their branding and positioning, our client gained far more market share by using a more diversified strategy, one that focused on both awareness campaigns and direct marketing strategies.

Our dental client had success because he carefully divided his marketing budget between longer-term concerns, like his general brand awareness, and shorter-term wins, like leads from direct marketing.

The Big Picture

The question, "Where do we start?" must inform a leader as to which things to address first. For leaders who know they've fallen behind in many areas of marketing and are looking for guidance on which area to begin focusing on, I suggest ordering your priorities as follows:

1. Create your position

How is your business different from its competition?

2. Articulate your business case

What business objective justifies this marketing budget?

3. Outline a go-to-market plan

What real-world experiences make up the customers' journeys that marketing must support?

4. A conversion methodology

As prospects become aware of our products/services, what experiences must they have in order to become customers?

a. What do they need to feel?

b. What do they need to know?

c. What obstacles must they overcome?
   (How must we remove decision friction?)

    d. How must we break down their overall conversion into bite-sized pieces?

    e. What's the thing that sells the thing?
(There could be more than one.)

5. Outline a connection plan

How will we continue to communicate with prospects?

    a. How will we stay in touch with people who become aware of our brand?

    b. How will we keep customers coming back?

    c. How can we leverage customer goodwill (reviews)?

6. Establish meaningful metrics

How will we measure the effectiveness of each awareness campaign?

7. Plan awareness methodologies and campaigns

How can we create effective awareness from targeted audiences?

Starting with the top of this list and working down, make sure there's at least a minimal amount of attention given to each relevant marketing concern before passing on to the next question or topic. While it isn't a fool-proof outline, I believe it's a spot-on marketing priority list that will be helpful for many small businesses.

CHAPTER SUMMARY

- Businesses commonly have more marketing needs than they're able to address with any one year's budget. Their leaders need to discern how to allocate their limited marketing budgets and what to prioritize.

- Smart leaders understand that some aspects of marketing require time to gain momentum, and they take a patient but persistent approach with a long-term vision.

- In the short term, leaders should direct a larger portion of their marketing budget toward their company's best business opportunity rather than each business segment equally.

- Leaders should prioritize the development of audience conversion strategies over awareness strategies.

- Leaders shouldn't put off gathering data. That's always a "year-one" activity.

- Leaders should balance longer-term marketing strategies with ones that bring short-term results.

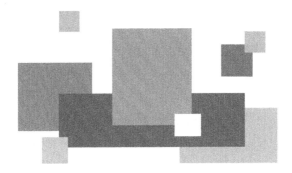

Final Thoughts
Marketing Leadership Matters

I remember it like it was yesterday. Samuel, owner of a custom furniture shop and veteran client of my agency stopped me in the hallway. "I need to tell you something," he said, sensing I was in a hurry. I stopped the obvious momentum I had toward my next meeting and made a deliberate effort to change my posture and my countenance from determined to unhurried and receptive. I sensed what he had to say was important to him.

"We had a pool party at my house last month," he said.

I had absolutely no idea where he was going with this, so I kept eye contact and nodded affirmingly so he'd continue, hoping he'd be brief.

"Because we had a good year, I was able to install that pool at our home, and it's been amazing for my family," he said. "And as I looked around at that party, I saw a lot of new faces. There were several new families blessed by my business's success."

Admittedly, I was beginning to wonder how long I'd be delayed with his personal anecdote. But then Samuel got down to what he really wanted to say.

"I have you to thank for this," he said, eyes welling up with tears.

Not understanding what he meant, I quickly deflected the compliment and reminded him how he had managed his company through that growth and that he deserved the credit, not me.

"No. You don't understand," he said. "You see, our website changed hosts last year, and there was a mistake that led to it being offline for a period of time. When the hosting company remedied it, a prior version of the site was made live by mistake, a prior version that didn't have your company's crucial improvements. Our sales leads stopped dead."

"My sales team tracked the history of our website leads before, during, and after this hosting glitch. Everyone at my company knows it was your company's work on our website, your investment in our marketing, that not only saved our business, but is still bringing in this unprecedented prosperity," he explained. "When your website was live, leads were pouring in. When the other version of the site was live, they stopped."

At this point, I had forgotten about my appointment, was completely drawn into his story, and was beginning to share Samuel's emotions regarding his success story.

"I'm thrilled to hear that," I responded. "But it's really my team that should get the credit. After all, I didn't work on your website."

"But there's something you're forgetting," he said. "When I first visited your company, you sat in on the sales meeting and gave me a vision for what successful marketing could do for my business. At the time, my business was failing. We had very little cash to invest. Your encouragement for us to invest in marketing was just what I needed, and I'm so glad I took your advice."

As I thanked him and walked to my next meeting, I had to put myself back together and dry my eyes. I thought about his story of the pool party and the tremendous feeling he must have had seeing his family, his employees, and their families enjoying the prosperity that business success brings. All of this was made possible because a leader had the vision to move forward with a good marketing plan.

Business success matters. And effective marketing leadership is the primary driver of business success. Samuel rose to the occasion and had an impact on his business, his family, his employees and their families, and his community. That impact will likely affect generations, opening doors for new college choices for his kids and his employees' kids, more secure retirement options for his company, and more resources for the local non-profits and places of worship Samuel supports.

As I wrap up these discussions on marketing leadership and the questions you can ask to help you become even more effective, I want to encourage you. I want you to understand just how important it is for you to continue to grow in this category of your leadership potential. I want you to consider the impact this decision and commitment will have on your business, your family, your team members, and your community. I want you to reflect, as Samuel did, on how far-reaching that success will be.

Not everyone is wired to be a brilliant marketer, but anyone can learn to ask 12 questions. In doing so, over time, you will join Samuel in celebrating astounding prosperity in your life and in the lives of those around you.

CONGRATULATIONS!

Having finished this book, you are set up to be an even
more effective marketing leader, empowered with
12 questions that will transform your thinking, the teams
you direct, and the organization you lead!

Want more? Get free downloads and other helpful
resources related to this book!
Visit **www.TheCrucial12.com**.

Learn more about the author and contact him by visiting
SteveWolgemuth.com.